EXTREME
COUPONING

EXTREME
COUPONING

LEARN HOW TO BE A SAVVY SHOPPER AND
SAVE MONEY . . . ONE COUPON AT A TIME

Joni Meyer-Crothers
with Beth Adelman

 NEW AMERICAN LIBRARY

New American Library
Published by the Penguin Group
Penguin Group (USA) Inc., 375 Hudson Street,
New York, New York 10014, USA
Penguin Group (Canada), 90 Eglinton Avenue East, Suite 700, Toronto,
Ontario M4P 2Y3, Canada (a division of Pearson Penguin Canada Inc.)
Penguin Books Ltd., 80 Strand, London WC2R 0RL, England
Penguin Ireland, 25 St. Stephen's Green, Dublin 2,
Ireland (a division of Penguin Books Ltd.)
Penguin Group (Australia), 707 Collins Street, Melbourne, Victoria 3008,
Australia (a division of Pearson Australia Group Pty. Ltd.)
Penguin Books India Pvt. Ltd., 11 Community Centre, Panchsheel Park,
New Delhi–110 017, India
Penguin Group (NZ), 67 Apollo Drive, Rosedale, Auckland 0632,
New Zealand (a division of Pearson New Zealand Ltd.)
Penguin Books (South Africa), Rosebank Office Park, 181 Jan Smuts Avenue,
Parktown North 2193, South Africa
Penguin China, B7 Jiaming Center, 27 East Third Ring Road North,
Chaoyang District, Beijing 100020, China

Penguin Books Ltd., Registered Offices:
80 Strand, London WC2R 0RL, England

Published by New American Library,
a division of Penguin Group (USA) Inc.

First New American Library Printing, March 2013
10   9   8   7   6

 REGISTERED TRADEMARK—MARCA REGISTRADA

LIBRARY OF CONGRESS CATALOGING-IN-PUBLICATION DATA:
Meyer-Crothers, Joni.
Extreme couponing: learn how to be a savvy shopper and save money . . .
one coupon at a time/Joni Meyer-Crothers with Beth Adelman.
p.   cm.
ISBN 978-0-451-41660-5
1. Shopping.   2. Coupons (Retail trade).   3. Consumer education.
4. Home economics.   I. Adelman, Beth.   II. Title.
TX335.M46 2013
640—dc23   2012038751

Set in Walbaum MT STD
Designed by Alissa Amell

Printed in the United States of America

PUBLISHER'S NOTE
While the author has made every effort to provide accurate telephone numbers, Internet
addresses, and other contact information at the time of publication, neither the publisher
nor the author assumes any responsibility for errors, or for changes that occur after
publication. Further, publisher does not have any control over and does not assume any
responsibility for author or third-party Web sites or their content.

CONTENTS

EXTREME
COUPONING

INTRODUCTION

When I was five years old, a missionary came and preached in our church about how many people in the United States and throughout the world are hungry. I still remember that service so vividly: I was sitting in the third pew, and I had on one of my Sunday church dresses and my little red shoes. He talked about how it was our responsibility to feed those hungry people, and I remember thinking to myself, I will. I'm going to help change the world by feeding the hungry. I wasn't sure how I was going to make a difference, especially at the age of five, but it was always something that was in my mind and heavy on my heart.

And then, twenty years ago, my children and I found ourselves among those hungry people, and feeding the hungry became very personal and real to me. I was going through a divorce, I had three young children, and for about six months *I could not feed them*. There were nights I gave up my food so my kids could have a little bit more. We were hungry and sometimes it was even worse than that. It wasn't like when you don't eat for twelve hours and you have hunger pangs—we were starving!

Thinking about that time is still so emotional for me (I'm actually tearing up as I write this), because I remember my children going to bed every night saying, "Mommy, we're hungry." It was devastating. A mom is supposed to take care of her children and provide for them. I just didn't know what I could do. I felt like I was letting my children down and was a failure as a parent.

It was a horrible, horrible time. It got so bad that I found myself having to make choices between toothpaste and feminine products. We couldn't afford to purchase both. I put tissue in my pants when I was on my monthly cycle so my kids could brush their teeth.

But I did keep praying. You know, I was never mad at God; I just didn't understand why I was going through that tough time. But I knew God had a plan for me and my children. I remember praying, "God, I don't know why I'm going through this, but when I get out of it I'm going to make a difference. I'm going to help others who are struggling, because nobody should have to make the choices I have to make; nobody should have to hear their children say, 'Mommy, I'm hungry.'"

After about six months, things got better for us. I got work doing some medical transcription out of my home, and with the extra money I could finally feed my children.

Two years later I met Jamie, and in 1996 we got married. After two miscarriages exactly one year apart, we decided to pursue adoption. We were blessed with four more wonderful children. Things were great for our family.

And then, about five years ago, Jamie lost his job. He worked in an automotive factory, and he got laid off when the economy went bad. The situation was not as desperate as it had been for me as a single mom twenty years ago, but we sure needed a way to stretch our dollars. My friend Rachel showed me two items I could get for free at the store using coupons. It was no big deal—just free Bisquick and Dole fruit cups. But it felt so *awesome* to know that I could actually walk out of the store with those items and not pay a penny for them by using coupons—simple pieces of paper that had never mattered much to me before. And, since I am a major overachiever, I thought, If there are two items I can get for free, there must be a lot more out there. I've got to figure this out. At that moment, *free* became one of my favorite words.

Within two weeks, we had more than three thousand dollars' worth of food for which we paid only a little over a hundred dollars. When I realized what I'd done, I thought, This isn't couponing, this is a ministry! I remembered what had been placed on my heart thirty-five years ago. This was my way to finally make a difference and help feed the hungry, and I was excited!

My husband and I decided to start an open pantry in our garage. We have a commercial freezer filled with meats, frozen vegetables, pizza, breakfast food, frozen dinners, and similar foods. We have a refrigerator filled with milk, butter, eggs, cheese, yogurt, dinner rolls, juice—the normal things you find in a refrigerator but that you typically can't get at a food bank. We also have two very large shelving units stocked with nonperishable food items, cleaning supplies, toilet paper, paper towels, tissues, laundry detergent, and toiletries, including many feminine care products and toothpaste—items that are very close to my heart!

We put the word out that anybody in our church and our community could come over any time, day or night, just let themselves into the garage and take what they need, no strings attached. I know from my own experience that if you go to a food bank, you feel scrutinized; plus, they limit what you can take. We want everyone to feel comfortable. All we ask is that, when they're in a better position, they pass the blessing on to others. Besides our own church and local community, occasionally other organizations and food banks contact us and we share our open pantry with them too. Thanks to couponing, we're currently getting about five thousand dollars' worth of groceries a month for about two hundred dollars, and we donate eighty percent of it. So it's not just couponing to me, it's definitely a ministry. Through couponing, we're able to help hundreds of people. And by teaching people what I know about couponing, we're able to help feed thousands more.

I've realized that if my family is able to make such a huge difference, with my husband still out of work, anyone can do this. *Anyone!* And while you're doing it, you can teach other people how to use coupons to stretch their dollars. I know there are many other families who are going through the same struggles I went through as a young single mom. And through the power of coupons, we really do have the ability to step up and make sure nobody goes hungry. It is all about passing the blessing on, with the hope that those who receive will keep the momentum going. It is my hope that this becomes a continuous cycle of grace and giving. This is my vision.

I understand that this is a lot to take on when you're just getting started in couponing. If you feel you need to start a little smaller, that's okay too. You can go as little or as big as you want. But at least take advantage of what you're offered. Think about how many times you get a coupon and throw it out. Maybe it's just for fifty or seventy-five cents, so you think, Why bother? Well, with just a few of those coupons you could save five dollars a week. Still not enough for you? When was the last time you went to the supermarket and bought yourself a really nice steak? Where I live, a good steak is twelve dollars a pound. In just seventeen days, you'd save enough for a pound of porterhouse. But believe me, you can do a lot better than that.

I wasn't looking for any recognition for my efforts to teach others my couponing techniques, and I certainly didn't expect to end up on national television. But in March 2011, I got a phone call from someone who identified herself as Kiran from Sharp Entertainment and asked me if I had ever heard of the show TLC *Extreme Couponing*. My two oldest daughters play pranks on me all the time, and they loved to tease me about my coupons, so I thought Kiran was some kid they'd gotten to mess with me. Kiran talked a long time, but I was only half listening to what she said because I kept expecting my daughters to burst in at any moment and say, "Ha-ha! We gotcha!" Finally I cut her off with a short "Why don't you shoot me an e-mail?"

Two minutes later an e-mail popped up from Sharp Entertainment. This was no joke. Three families from our church had nominated us to be on the show. I told Kiran we needed the weekend to really pray about it before making any commitment.

I finally decided I'd do it, but with two conditions. I'd never been on television before, but I knew that sometimes "reality" shows are only partly real. So the first condition was that I would be portrayed exactly as I am; they couldn't make me say or do things that just aren't me. The second condition was that a hundred percent of what we bought on the show by couponing had to be donated, and they had to show that on the air. They agreed.

Three weeks later, film crews showed up. Over the next seven months, my family and I filmed four episodes of *Extreme Couponing,* plus a Black Friday special where we showed viewers how to get the best prices, as well as "door buster" specials. We even got to teach our producer, Nicole, why door buster deals are called door busters. (Because they are such good deals that everyone is waiting at the doors to bust in.) She had never been out shopping on Black Friday before.

Along the way, Jamie showed off some pretty sweet dance moves, I made up a few words, and we had a ton of fun (I'll tell you all my stories in the book). But the biggest highlight of all was that in just four episodes on *Extreme Couponing,* I donated fourteen thousand dollars' worth of products that cost me just forty-five dollars (all in sales tax), plus another ten thousand dollars from the Black Friday special that only cost two thousand; everything went to less fortunate families for Christmas.

I spend a lot of my time going around to church groups and teaching classes on couponing, so I've heard all the reasons people come up with for why they can't start couponing. The first one is always "It takes too much time to get organized." Yes, initially it might take you a couple of hours to get organized and figure out how you are going to do it. But there are tricks to getting organized quickly. (I'll show you how in this book.) And it's so worth it; once you have everything in place, you can save thousands and thousands of dollars and also help people in need.

One of the main strategies I advocate is stocking up on items (I'll explain how that works in the book). People always ask me, "Why do you have to buy ten or twenty of something? Why do you have to take it to those extremes?" The answer is that if an item is free, it is usually not going to be on sale again for another eight or twelve weeks. Why would you want to get it free one week and then pay full price for it the next eleven weeks? It just makes sense to stock up.

Another thing I hear a lot is that you can't get healthy food with coupons. But that's just not true. There are many items you can get with coupons that are super healthy, including organic foods and fresh produce. Plus, you can cut down what you pay for your cleaning supplies and toiletries by at least seventy-five percent—leaving you more money to shop at the organic grocery store. There are so many ways to be creative to save the most money.

Because I talk about couponing as a ministry, people also ask me about what happens to the workers at the supermarket and at the companies issuing the coupons. Does couponing mean those workers earn less money?

The answer, I am glad to say, is no. The manufacturers have a marketing budget that covers the costs of every coupon they issue. They want you to try their products. And if the manufacturers didn't offer coupons, they know most people would just buy the store brand or the cheapest brand. So they figure they're still coming out ahead if you buy their product but pay seventy-five cents or a dollar less. It's really smart business for the manufacturers.

It doesn't hurt the store either. For each coupon we use, the store gets reimbursed for the value of the coupon, plus an eight-cent handling fee. So the store is actually making more money when people coupon than when they don't!

I know from my own experience that couponing sometimes means the difference between your family being hungry and not being hungry. But what if you're not struggling to feed your children? What if you're just a middle-class family who's not rich but not hungry either?

Honestly, there's no reason everybody shouldn't be couponing, no matter what social or economic class you're in, because it's going to free up a lot of your money. My sister is a perfect example. She and her family were getting by okay, but they didn't have the means to take vacations or do some of the other special things that many families do. When she started couponing, it freed up a lot of money so that now they're able to afford some things they couldn't before. For example, they are able to take minivacations and go to the movies and out to nice restaurants—things they didn't have the money for before she started couponing.

I think you can see by now that for every reason you can think of *not* to coupon, I can think of at least two reasons why you should. As I said before, couponing is a ministry for me. With this book, I want to teach you how to save money. But I also want to teach you how to share with other people through your savings and how to give back. So it's a win-win for everybody. Not only are you being blessed, but through couponing you are passing the blessing on to others.

CHAPTER 1

What's Your Spending Situation?

Before Jamie lost his job, there were times when I spent money almost without thinking. My downfall was fountain drinks. I do love my diet soda. Whenever I stopped for gas, I also picked up a drink. Then I'd look around the store and say to myself, "I think I need some gum. And chips. And maybe some candy." I'd swipe my debit card to pay for it all, spending ten to fifteen dollars (on top of the gas, of course), and I did that maybe twice a week. Without my realizing it, that seemingly minor impulse spending added up to between eighty and a hundred dollars a month—nine hundred and sixty to twelve hundred dollars a year.

At that time, we never really thought a great deal about our spending, and we certainly never made a budget. The money came in, and the money went out. We paid our bills, and with any money left over, we'd put some in the bank and have fun with the rest. The economy was good and we didn't think the future would be much different.

Then, in 2007, Jamie got laid off, and we realized we had to reevaluate our financial situation. For us, the path to saving money began when we became more conscious of our spending. That was our first step to getting a handle on our finances. I only wish we had realized it years ago.

Begin with a Budget

Almost everyone knows what they spend every month on large, fixed expenses such as insurance, car payments, rent or mortgage. Maybe you also put away a set amount every month in a savings account, a college fund, or to pay your taxes. But I bet you would be surprised to see the breakdown of how, when, and where you spend your discretionary cash. This is why I advise you to write down exactly what you spend in a month. Then make the time to take a look at those numbers. I was talking with a friend of mine who told me she thought she spent about a hundred dollars a month going out to eat. But when she looked at her restaurant receipts for thirty days, it added up to three hundred and fifty dollars. She had no idea she was spending that much!

This is why I believe a budget is so important. We've gotten so accustomed to using our debit card that often we don't even check the total. It may seem like just a couple of dollars every time you swipe your card, which is easily forgotten. But when you actually keep track of everything you spend, it can be a rude awakening.

So let's get started. First, write down how much you think you spend each month in just a couple of areas, and then at the end of thirty days, compare it to what you actually do spend. On page 21 I've given you a quick budget checklist. You'll see it's divided into seven categories: food, personal hygiene products, cleaning supplies, pets, entertainment, car, and personal. I've left out the big-ticket items, like rent or house payments, car payments, insurance, and going to the doctor, because you can't use coupons for those things.

Cash or Debit?

Why is it so important to track your spending for a month? Among other things, it helps you stop and realize how many times you use your debit card without thinking about it. Once you examine how often that happens, you may decide you really shouldn't be using it. It's just too easy to lose track of what you spend. The debit card is the main reason most people underestimate their spending and end up being surprised with the results of this budget exercise. That's why I pay for most of my transactions in cash.

I use what I call the envelope system. I have envelopes for each of our different budget categories, and each month I put a specific amount of cash in each envelope. As an envelope runs low, I know I have to cut back in that area, or take money from a less vital area (say, entertainment) to pay for a more vital area (like groceries).

Monthly Expenses		
	Estimated Spending	Actual Spending
Food		
Hygiene products (soap, shampoo, toothpaste, deodorant, toilet paper, etc.)		
Cleaning supplies (dish soap, paper towels, laundry detergent, etc.)		
Pets (pet food, supplies, grooming)		
Car (gas)		
Entertainment (restaurants, movies, concerts, sporting events, etc.)		
Personal (clothing, hair, nails, etc.)		

Now start on the first day of the month and keep track of everything you spend. You'll probably need a daily list for that. On page 22 is one that will get you through the first week (you can just make a copy for each week in the month).

I know it's a big task to keep track of everything for a whole month. The easiest way for me—and for most people—is to do it right away. Make sure you get receipts

Weekly Expenses

	Sunday	Monday	Tuesday	Wednesday	Thursday	Friday	Saturday	Total
Food								
Hygiene products (soap, shampoo, toothpaste, deodorant, toilet paper, etc.)								
Cleaning supplies (dish soap, paper towels, laundry detergent, etc.)								
Pets (pet food, supplies, grooming)								
Car (gas)								
Entertainment (restaurants, movies, concerts, sporting events, etc.)								
Personal (clothing, hair, nails, etc.)								

for everything you buy, and at the end of each day, take a few minutes to write it all down on your chart or enter it into a spreadsheet on your computer. Or you can carry a little notepad around with you and just write all your purchases down in that.

Add up your spending every week, and at the end of the month, calculate your totals and compare them to your monthly spending predictions. Most people are flabbergasted when they see how much they really spend. I know I was.

So how does this budget analysis fit in with couponing? Most people think couponing is just for groceries. But couponing can help out with pet food and pet supplies, personal hygiene products, cleaning supplies, and other items. So think paper towels, laundry detergent, shampoo, pain reliever, nail polish remover—all of it. That's why the budget is so important. Remember when I said you could start small? Take a look at any one or two categories where you were really shocked at how much you spend in a month. This is where you might start couponing.

Let's say you're surprised to find you're spending two hundred dollars a month on cleaning supplies and the same amount on personal hygiene products. Together, that's four hundred dollars a month. Multiply that by twelve months and you're spending forty-eight hundred dollars a year. But by using the couponing techniques I outline in this book, you will be able to get most of those products for free. Yes, I said *free*. So you'll have forty-eight hundred dollars to spend on other things! When you look at the bigger picture instead of week by week, that's when you have the aha moment: This is a lot bigger than what it looks like initially. But it all starts with that budget and seeing how much you spend each month.

So let's start small. Take one month and one category, and just concentrate on that. Pretty soon, you're going to think, Okay, this is pretty easy. Now I need to expand my savings to other categories. Even starting slowly, one step at a time, you'll see how coupons can really make a difference.

What If I'm Receiving Food Assistance?

You can still use coupons. Bring your coupons and your food assistance card to the supermarket check-out. They'll scan all your coupons, and then they'll swipe your food assistance card to pay for whatever is left. So let's say you have a coupon for a dollar off orange juice and the orange juice costs a dollar twenty-five. Your food assistance card will be charged the twenty-five-cent difference—and look, you just saved a dollar on one item.

This is going to free up a lot of money that you can use to buy your cleaning supplies and toiletries, which are not covered under food assistance and that maybe you couldn't afford before. I know too that many people run out of food assistance at the end of the month because it's really not enough. But couponing will stretch that food assistance budget for you.

continued ...

The best part, to me, is that you can use your savings to get you through the month and maybe even give something back. I got an e-mail recently from someone who receives food assistance and attended one of my classes. She used to have to go to the local food bank toward the end of the month because her monthly benefit ran out. Since she started couponing, she's still going to the food bank at the end of the month, but now it's to donate food to help others in need. That's what's so awesome about couponing.

This Is for Everyone (Yes, Everyone)

Some people struggle to make ends meet. Some people live paycheck to paycheck. Some people have the basics of what they need but would like to be able to put something aside for a rainy day or a family vacation. And some people have what they need, financially. Budgeting—and then couponing—is for everyone, regardless of your circumstances.

I think it's clear how budgeting and couponing will help if you're struggling to feed your family. But let's talk about how it will help those who have a good job with a steady income. Sometimes even people who have a regular paycheck have unforeseen expenses. What if there's a death in the family, an illness, or a decrease in salary? Isn't it better to be prepared ahead of time than to wait until it happens? With the power of coupons, you can prepare yourself now. By keeping track of what you spend, making a budget, and using coupons, you will stretch your dollar beyond what you need, giving you extra at the end of the month. I sure hope nothing bad happens to you, but if that little extra goes into a savings account every month, you can be prepared just in case an emergency does arise.

Couponing is such an easy way to save money. Most people in an average year are going to save between six thousand and ten thousand dollars just using the basic couponing strategies I'm sharing with you. I like to tell people it's like getting a huge pay raise.

The Thrill of the Challenge

One of my Facebook followers is a physician, and she's married to an attorney. This is a family that definitely doesn't need to coupon to make ends meet. Yet she's a serious couponer. She said it's become a hobby for her, because she likes the thrill of saving all that money. There is definitely a sense of satisfaction from going to the store with nothing but five dollars and a handful of coupons and coming home with bags and bags of groceries.

It reminds me of the first time I sent my husband, Jamie, to the supermarket, after I discovered extreme couponing. He thought I had gone off the deep end, but I insisted that he learn how to play the "coupon game." So I sent him with a stack of coupons, a twenty-dollar bill, and a grocery list that totaled over three hundred and fifty dollars' worth of food.

Now, Jamie is pretty laid-back; he never gets nervous or worked up. But when he got in the checkout line with an overloaded cart of groceries (that he'd stacked in his very neat way—it would have been two carts if I'd packed it) and just twenty dollars in his pocket, he was thinking, I'm going to look like such a fool if this couponing thing doesn't work.

But you know what? He ended up strutting out of the store with change from that twenty-dollar bill in his pocket. It's like a game, a challenge. How much can I get and how much can I save? There's absolutely a thrill in this kind of game.

If you're on a very tight budget, you will find that pretty soon you'll have extra money for the things you couldn't do before. You might decide to build a stockpile (more about that in chapter 8), or you might choose to splurge on something you previously couldn't afford— maybe a night at the movies or a fancy restaurant. A lot of people use the money they're saving through couponing to go on vacations. I've heard from couponers that they are now able to get their kids Christmas or birthday gifts they couldn't afford before, when all of that money was going for groceries. Others have told me they use the extra cash to buy their kids' school supplies and school clothes, and find they're no longer stressed about back-to-school time.

Remember, it starts with a budget, because we all need to know what we have coming in and what we have going out, no matter how much money we make.

For my own family, our budget shows us how much we can donate to our community. That's our number-one priority. But number two, even with Jamie still out of work, is doing fun activities with our kids that we couldn't otherwise afford. We used to spend twelve hundred dollars a month on groceries, and now we spend only two hundred a month. That's an extra thousand dollars a month! Recently we took the kids to a hotel with a water park. We are pretty frugal and don't usually spend money on things like that—the weekend cost us four hundred dollars—but it was fun to be able to splurge, and we didn't take *any* money away from our budget. The freedom we found through couponing gave us access to that money.

I think back to the times when I used to swipe my debit card at convenience stores, and how much money I just threw away. Now I'd rather use a coupon to get a free twenty-ounce soda, pour it into my own cup of ice, and save the bucks. All it took was me waking up and realizing that I really had no idea how much money we were spending.

I also want to challenge you to share your savings and share your blessing. Take some of your savings and give to a local food bank, a charity, or a neighbor or a family member. Everyone knows someone who is in need or could use help. It doesn't matter who you give to—*just give.*

Of course, you can donate some of the money you've saved. But if you use the couponing techniques you'll learn here, you can give so much more. For example, if you're stockpiling cereal because you can get it for free this week, pick up twenty boxes for yourself but remember to also pick up a couple of extra boxes to donate.

I know a lot of people are thinking, We're just barely getting by ourselves, so how can I give back and help somebody else? But by using coupons, you are getting items for free or, at the very least, really cheap, and that gives you the freedom to be able to help others who are in need. It's such a good feeling, because suddenly what you thought wasn't possible *is* possible. You know, it's kind of empowering to suddenly have that ability to give back. I think most people do want to help, but they just don't have the means. Couponing will really open that door for you, so you can help a lot of people.

So I challenge you to donate five items a week. Just five. Give them to a local food bank, a shelter, or someone you know who is in need. You don't have to spend any money; all you have to do is take a little piece of paper with you when you go to the grocery store—something you're already doing. If every single person who reads this book donates five items a week, lives will be changed, just through the power of coupons.

Takeaway Tip$

How Much Money Can I Save by Couponing?

Most people, in an average year, are going to save between six thousand and ten thousand dollars just doing basic couponing.

How Much Time Is This Really Going to Take Me Each Week?

A lot of people think they are not going to save a lot of money with couponing once you factor in the amount of time it takes. Yes, your time is worth something. But even if you go full on, couponing and using the Internet and everything else I am going to teach you in this book, you are only going to spend a few hours a week—and you are going to save six thousand, ten thousand, twelve thousand dollars a year.

continued . . .

Can I Use My Food Assistance Card with Coupons?

Yes. You can use your food assistance to pay for whatever grocery bill is left after you've used all your coupons.

Isn't Couponing Just for People Who Are Struggling to Get By?

If you can give yourself a six-thousand-to-ten-thousand-dollar raise over the year, why wouldn't you? Couponing is for everybody because it frees up money for you to spend on other things.

CHAPTER 2

Collecting as Many Coupons as You Can

Your local Sunday newspaper usually includes inserts that are full of coupons—since you bought this book, you probably already know that. Maybe you also get those bundles of store circulars that are full of sales announcements and store coupons. Are you really going to sit down and cut out all those coupons? The answer is yes! And if you're an extreme couponer, that's just scratching the surface.

When it comes to couponing, more is definitely better. You want to collect as many coupons as you can. The reason for this is something I call the sale cycle. The way to get the most value from your coupons is to buy a product with a coupon when it's on sale, and most products go on sale about every eight to twelve weeks. If you have only one or two coupons for that product, you won't be able to buy enough to last you until it goes on sale again. You'll be stuck paying full price until the sale cycle comes around again. And the whole point of extreme couponing is *never* to pay full price!

So my first advice is to make sure you have enough coupons to get what you need for at least twelve weeks. If your family goes through one box of cereal in a week, you want to have at least twelve coupons to shop with, so you can stock up until it goes on sale again. (Actually, for a lot of products, such as cereal, packaged foods, hygienic products, cleaning supplies, and laundry detergent, I recommend buying enough for six months or even a year if the products will keep that long. More about that in chapter 8.)

In addition to the twelve-week sale cycle, there's an annual sales cycle for many items. Some of them are obvious: Halloween candy goes on clearance right after Halloween every year. But there are others too: January is National Oatmeal Month, March is National Frozen Food Month, and National Pet Week is in May. You'll find great sales to go along with these promotions, when certain products hit rock-bottom prices. For example, National Baby Safety Month is September, so that would be a great time to get baby food and diapers at the best prices. Sure, you can find them on sale throughout the year, but in September they are going to be the very cheapest, and that's when you want to really build your stockpile for those products. (You'll find a list of seasonal sale and clearance items below.) Yes, initially you might have to put a little bit of money into stocking up, but in the long run you are going to be saving a lot more. So it's important to have as many coupons as possible to get you through. Fortunately, there are plenty of places where you can get coupons. Let's look at them.

The Seasonal Sale Cycle			
Month	Foods on Sale	Seasonal Sale Items	Clearance Items
January	Diet foods (Healthy Choice, Lean Cuisine, etc.), soups, snack foods, soda, oatmeal, tea, eggs, granola bars, diet shakes/drinks, Kashi, 100-calorie packs, chips, dips	Cold medicines, cough syrup, diet products, exercise equipment, furniture, organizational items/shelving, pain relief, vitamins, white sales	Christmas decorations, coats, New Year's Eve party supplies, toys, winter boots, winter clothing

continued . . .

The Seasonal Sale Cycle

Month	Foods on Sale	Seasonal Sale Items	Clearance Items
February	Bacon, canned goods, crackers, hash browns, hot breakfast products, oatmeal, pancake mix, sausages, snacks, soda, soy sauce, stir-fry mixes, syrup, teriyaki sauce, veggie trays, waffles	Candles, cards, chocolate, flowers, KY jelly	Valentine's Day products (after the fourteenth)
March	Frozen foods, juice concentrates, frozen vegetables, cheese, crackers, corned beef, ham, eggs	Cleaning supplies, Easter baskets, Easter candy, Easter clothing, Easter decorations	Winter clothing, snow shovels, snow blowers, sledding supplies
April	Baking products, eggs, ham, organic and natural foods, refrigerated cookie dough, spices	Batteries, carbon monoxide monitors, CFL and LED lights, dyeing kits, FREE items on Tax Day, gardening equipment, personal care products, reusable shopping bags, seeds, spring cleaning supplies	Easter decorations, Easter baskets, egg dyeing kits

The Seasonal Sale Cycle

Month	Foods on Sale	Seasonal Sale Items	Clearance Items
May	Canned beans, condiments, frozen Mexican entrees and snacks, grilling/cookout meat, hamburger/hot dog buns, salad dressing, salsa, shredded cheese, snacks, soda, tortilla chips, tortillas	Allergy medication, baby diapers/wipes, beach toys, bird feeders, candles, charcoal, dog and cat food, flowers, grills, insect repellent, jewelry, lawn mowers, mulch, paper products, utensils, etc., patio furniture, perfumes, pool equipment, seeds, soil, sunscreen	None
June	Butter, cheese, condiments, eggs, hamburgers/hot dogs/grilling meats, hamburger/hot dog buns, ice cream, milk, salad dressing, yogurt	Pool equipment, pool toys, BBQ grills, charcoal, sunscreen, insect repellant, paper products, plastic utensils	None
July	Baked beans, BBQ sauce, charcoal, chips, condiments, dips, grilling meats, hamburger/hot dog buns, juices, soda	Back-to-school supplies, backpacks, insect repellent, sunscreen	Fourth of July items

continued . . .

The Seasonal Sale Cycle

Month	Foods on Sale	Seasonal Sale Items	Clearance Items
August	Cereal, food items for lunches (juice boxes, lunch meat, Lunchables, pudding cups, snacks)	Backpacks, disinfecting wipes, hand sanitizers, lunchboxes, school clothing, school supplies, shoes, plastic food storage bags	BBQ items, camping equipment, charcoal, fans, gardening tools, insect repellent, patio furniture, pool equipment, seeds, summer clothing, sunscreen, swimsuits
September	Lunch box foods	Baby products, restaurant deals, school clothing, school supplies (through Labor Day), shoes	Air conditioners, back-to-school supplies (after Labor Day), BBQ supplies, camping supplies, pool equipment
October	Baking products, candy, canned pumpkin, cookies, evaporated milk, lobster, nuts, pie crusts, shrimp	Costumes, fire prevention equipment, Halloween accessories, pet foods, pet toys, pet treats, pink products (for Breast Cancer Awareness), smoke alarms	None

The Seasonal Sale Cycle

Month	Foods on Sale	Seasonal Sale Items	Clearance Items
November	Baking goods, boxed potato products, broth, cake and brownie mixes, canned foods (soups, vegetables, fruits, etc.), canned pumpkin, chocolate chips, frozen pies, gelatin, gravy mixes, spaghetti sauce, stuffing, tea and coffee, turkey	Smoking cessation products, blankets, electronics, clothing, coats, toys, appliances, Black Friday door buster deals	Halloween products (costumes, etc.), Halloween party favors, Halloween candy
December	Baking supplies, bread/rolls, deli platters, eggnog, flour, frozen pies, gravy mixes, ham, muffin, cake, and brownie mixes, pie fillings, snacks, soda, soups, sour cream, stuffing, sugar	After-Christmas sales, fall decorations, holiday decorations, paper goods, toys	After-Christmas sales, beginning December 26, but January 1 they will be the cheapest!

In the Newspapers

The most obvious place to get your coupons is the Sunday newspaper. There may not be inserts on holiday weekends, such as Memorial Day and Labor Day, but otherwise, every Sunday you'll find them in your local newspaper. I encourage you to pick up one copy of the paper for every member of your family. Maybe you're thinking, If I'm spending two dollars for every newspaper, am I really saving money? Well, you'll save a lot more than two dollars when you put all those coupons to work! But let's go ahead and think outside the box. Where can you get additional inserts? Start asking around and find out who throws those inserts away and might be willing to give them to you instead. Ask family members, church members, even the parents at your kids' school.

Another great resource is nursing homes and assisted-living facilities; most of the residents there subscribe to the newspapers but don't use the coupons because their meals are taken care of. If you go in and talk to the manager, he or she might agree to let you set up a box in the front for residents to drop off their inserts. Then you can go in once a week and pick up the coupons from all the residents who aren't using them. Of course, be sure to ask the manager's permission before you do anything like that. If you are donating some of what you get with your coupons to a food bank or other charity, let the manager know. But please, don't say you are if you aren't. And while you're there, it wouldn't hurt to go around and thank the residents who donated—you might brighten their day with a little visit!

Do you live in an apartment building? If your municipality requires paper recycling, there's a designated place where people drop off their newspapers for collection. Anything that's in the recycling pile is basically someone else's trash, and you can certainly pick out the coupon inserts. (Of course, you should never go through other people's trash cans in front of their homes. In some places, that's even illegal.) I have some friends who live in apartment buildings that don't recycle, but residents do drop off their Sunday coupon inserts near the mailboxes for whoever wants them. If someone leaves them up for grabs, take advantage— it's not costing you a penny.

The Magazine for Coupons

Lots of magazines include coupons and special offers, especially the magazines that focus on homemaking, such as *Good Housekeeping* and *Woman's Day*. But there's a magazine called *All You* that's filled with coupons. There are some good articles in it about how to save money, but the best part of the magazine is that it has very high-value coupons, and lots of them. It usually sells for two dollars (and at that price, it's worth it), but you can shop around on the Internet for magazine subscription deals and end up paying between fifty cents and one dollar an issue.

In Circulars

Most of the supermarket and drugstore chains also put out weekly sale circulars, and they are filled with great coupons. Here's a tip that a lot of people don't know: Some of the coupons in these flyers are manufacturer's coupons, not store coupons. Take a close look at each coupon; if it says "Manufacturer's Coupon," it can be used at any store that accepts manufacturers' coupons—even if the coupon has a store logo printed on it. If it says "Manufacturer's Coupon," you don't have to go to the store that sent the circular; just cut the coupon out and use it at a different store. And that's an awesome way to save a lot of money.

There's a grocery store that's about fifty miles from my home; I don't shop there often, but I still get their flyers. They always have very high-value coupons in their store paper, but because they are manufacturers' coupons, we can clip them out and use them anywhere. What's the advantage of using the coupon at a different store? Well, aside from the fact that I don't always want to drive fifty miles to shop, that store is very small, so their prices are almost twice what they are in the big supermarket chains. A seventy-five-cents-off coupon at that store is really not going to get me big savings. But I can take the coupon to one of our local supermarkets that doubles coupons, meaning a seventy-five-cent coupon would become a dollar fifty off on a product that's priced lower in the first place. I might even end up getting that product for free—and remember, one of my favorite words is *free*.

So always take a look at the top of the coupon to see if it's a store or a manufacturer's coupon. The store coupon can be used only in that store, but the manufacturer's coupon can be used anywhere.

From the Manufacturer

You can sometimes get coupons directly from the manufacturer. Just find the company's Web site by typing it into any search engine (in chapter 10 we'll talk about the Swagbucks search engine). You'll end up on the company's home page. Somewhere on the page, usually across the top or the bottom (or sometimes both), you'll find a link that says "Contact Us" or something similar. Go ahead and click on it. Often you'll end up with a lot of contact options, for job openings, for information, and so on. . . . I always pick "compliments."

Write an e-mail saying you'd like to try their product,

or that you did try it and really loved it. The funny thing is, if you come right out and ask for coupons, they won't send any. But if you tell them you'd like to try their product, they'll sometimes send you coupons.

One of the ladies in my blog community likes organic foods, which are pretty expensive. So she sent an e-mail to one of her favorite manufacturers and said, "I really like your products but they are very expensive. Even so, I would like to continue on an organic diet." They sent her ten coupons for two dollars off on various organic foods. Pretty easy, right?

You can't write to the same manufacturer every week, because they won't send you coupons that often. But try it every six months, and most manufacturers will keep sending you coupons. Obviously, they hope you are going to continue to buy their product even when the coupons run out. Maybe you will and maybe you won't, but don't worry about the company. The value of the coupons is figured right in to their marketing budget and they'll be fine either way.

Stores Do It Too

A lot of the big chain stores have Web sites where you can print coupons. Target, Meijer, and Rite Aid are just some of the ones that do. If there are stores where you especially like to shop, take a look at their Web sites to see if they offer coupons.

Many manufacturers also have promotion programs you can sign up for. These often include sweepstakes, coupons, and special offers. Take a look at some of the things you like to buy and note who makes them. Let's say you notice a lot of the cereal you buy is from Kellogg's, or your toiletries tend to be from Procter & Gamble, or you like cleaning supplies from Arm & Hammer. All of these companies have promotional programs. Use your search engine to find their Web sites on the Internet, then look for a link that says "offers" or "promotions" or "savings"—something like that.

Go ahead and sign up. They'll usually send you a coupon right away, and then as more coupons become available, they will e-mail you. These are usually coupons you print off the Internet, using your own printer. (You don't need anything special to print them.) Couponing bloggers (more about that world in chapter 6) will also let you know when new Internet printables come out from the big companies. Those are usually high-value coupons too.

The one thing you should know about signing up for promotional programs is that your e-mail in-box will quickly fill up with junk mail, so you probably want to set up a separate "coupon" mailbox with a different e-mail address than your personal one. If your Internet provider doesn't allow you to set up more than one e-mail address, get one through one of the free e-mail services, such as Gmail, Hotmail, or Yahoo. Use it just for your couponing activities. Since there will be offers you really want mixed in with all the spam, remember to check your "coupon" mailbox regularly.

From the Internet

There are a number of sites on the Internet that gather up manufacturers' coupons and let you print them right off the site. Some of the ones I use are RedPlum.com, Smart-Source.com, Coupons.com, and CouponNetwork.com. They offer new coupons at the beginning of every month, and then add one or two more offers just about every day.

Most sites let you print a maximum of two coupons for each product from the same computer. But if you have, say, three computers in your home, you can print two from each computer and get a total of six. Cool, right? I have another secret for you. CouponBug.com is another site that has all the same coupons as Coupons.com. From CouponBug.com, you can print one additional coupon. So on Coupons.com you can print two and then you can print one more from CouponBug.com. You can also go to your local library or community center and print coupons from their computers. Couponing math is all about multiplication.

Extreme Couponers Never Copy Coupons

It's okay to print as many coupons as you can. But it is *never* okay to put an Internet printable coupon (or any other coupon) on a copy machine and photo-copy it. When you print multiples of the same coupon, they're not exactly the same. The number at the top of the coupon changes. Take a look at the coupons you print out and you'll see that each one has a unique number.

When you photocopy a coupon, obviously, the number at the top stays the same. The store will get reimbursed from the manufacturer for the original coupon, but not for the copies. So essentially, what you are doing is stealing from the store. That's why it is one hundred percent illegal to copy coupons. It's also not ethical.

It hurts other shoppers too. When a store accepts fraudulent coupons, it doesn't get reimbursed and it loses money. That forces the store to raise prices for all its customers. And eventually, if they've been burned enough, stores may stop accepting Internet printable coupons altogether. That's why extreme couponers never copy coupons.

On the Product

Sometimes coupons pop up right where you need them: on the product itself. We've all seen those packages with bright stickers that say "Instant Coupon." You peel the sticker off at the register and get your instant savings. That's always a manufacturer's coupon, so sometimes you can combine it with a store coupon for even bigger savings.

Sometimes, though, the coupon is printed on the package itself or is tucked inside. Is it okay to cut the coupon out of the box or open it and pull out the coupon? Absolutely— if you're buying the item, of course! Obviously, it's not all right to cut it out, take the coupon, and leave the box. But as long as you are actually buying that item, you can cut or open the box if you want to. You do not have to take that product home and then cut the coupon out and use it the next time! What if the product isn't on sale the next time you go to the store? You'd be missing an opportunity to maximize your savings.

I always take a pair of scissors with me when I go shopping, just to cut out coupons. People laugh at me, but it's a great way to save money, especially if the item is on sale. For example, we recently found some cereal that was on sale for two dollars (usually it's $3.89). There was also an eighty-cents-off coupon on the outside of the box, and the store doubled coupons, so that was worth a dollar sixty to me. If I hadn't had my scissors, I would have spent two dollars on the cereal; instead, I bought it for only forty cents! Holla!

In the Store

Another way coupons come along right when and where you need them is in the store, where you'll find tear pads, blinkies, and peelies. (I promise, all this lingo will be reviewed in chapter 4!)

Peelies are the peel-off stickers on the packages that I talked about in the previous section. Tear pads are big pads of coupons that are usually stuck on the shelf next to a product. Often you'll find them in convenience stores, like the ones at gas stations. You tend to see tear pads when manufacturers are bringing out a new product or a new version of a product, and they want you to give it a try. Those are usually very high-value coupons, to really tempt you.

Be considerate and take only enough coupons to cover the items you are buying. So if you plan to buy two, then take just two coupons. Leave some for the next couponer. You can use them at any store that accepts manufacturers' coupons.

Blinkies are more often found in grocery stores. They're those little coupon-dispensing machines that are stuck to the shelves in front of the products. These too are often very high-value coupons. Obviously, I wouldn't stand there and take all of them out, but do take enough to cover all the products you are buying.

They're called blinkies because they usually have a little blinking light on them. When I first saw one, I thought the light was a motion sensor—like the faucets and paper towel dispensers in public restrooms—and that you had to wave your hand in front of it to get another coupon. So I'd stand there waving and swaying back and forth and basically doing a blinkie dance until another coupon came out.

One day I was shopping with my friend Danielle, and when she saw me doing the blinkie dance she looked at me like I was nuts. I explained what I was doing, and she started to laugh. She told me blinkies dispense a new coupon every thirty seconds. All I had to do was pull one out, wait thirty seconds, and another one would appear. No dancing required.

But sometimes I do the dance anyway, just for fun.

With a Savings Card

Most supermarket, drugstore, and gas station chains have savings or loyalty cards that you can sign up for. Every time you shop there, they scan your card at the register and your savings are automatically calculated. You should have a savings card at every store in your area; it's well worth it. They cost nothing, and you can save a lot. Yes, you do have to give them your address and e-mail, but they use that information to tell you about what's on sale and send you coupons and other offers, so this is not a bad thing. (Use your "coupon" e-mail address for this). Stores with savings card programs usually won't give you the sale price on an item unless you scan your card, so make sure to have it with you.

These cards are often linked to programs that offer additional perks. For example, many calculate "points" on each of your purchases that translate into dollars off on future purchases, or even free gasoline. Be sure to check your register receipt every time you go, because the points and their expiration date will be printed on it. Savings card holders also get exclusive store coupons printed on their receipt. And sometimes you can load coupons on your savings card in advance (I'll explain how in the next section on cell phones).

It's smart to keep your savings cards with you at all times. Even if you don't plan to stop at a specific store, you may pass it on your way somewhere else and notice that they're having an awesome sale.

Savings card programs always come with one credit-card-size card and two small ones to put on a key chain. I have all of mine dangling from my key chain so I always have them with me. But Jamie doesn't like all those cards hanging from his keys, so he's taken all the small ones and put them on their own key ring. When he goes out, he pockets his keys plus the key ring with the savings cards.

On Your Cell Phone

Many grocery store chains participate in e-offers, which are coupons you can load onto your cell phone or your store savings card. These offers are available through the Web site CellFire.com. (Cell Fire also has some printable coupons, so it's definitely worth a visit.) Just register at Cell Fire by entering your zip code and the number of each store savings card you have. Then they will show you the stores in your area that have e-offers. Click on the coupons you want and they are automatically loaded onto your savings card. When you check out, the register will apply your coupons when the cashier scans your card. So it's like a paper coupon, except it's on your card.

Cell Fire also has a free app for just about every kind of cell phone that lets you use your phone to browse coupons and add them to your savings card. You can also download nongrocery coupons for clothing, toys, or furniture onto your cell phone and just show your mobile coupon to the cashier to get your discount.

The only problem with e-offers is that stores will not

double them. So if you are going to a store that doubles paper coupons, you'll do better with a hard copy. Using an e-offer for, say, a fifty-cent coupon will only get you fifty cents off, while a fifty-cent paper coupon would get you a dollar off.

Not every store with a savings card participates in e-offers, but there are a lot, so look around. National retailers such as Meijer and many regional supermarket chains participate in these programs, and you can get e-offers right from their Web sites. Sometimes they're called digital coupons or e-coupons—no matter what they're called, they all work the same way.

One of our local supermarket chains has such a generous e-offer program that if you forget your cell phone, you can enter the phone number at the store and it will recognize what coupons you put on the cell phone and deduct them that way too. So even without your phone or card, you get the savings. Now, that's good service!

Just remember: If you have a store that doubles coupons, always use your manufacturer's coupon first, and then use the other sources, which won't double.

On eBay

You can get just about everything on eBay, including coupons. These are manufacturers' coupons that some enterprising person has clipped from the local newspaper inserts, and they usually come in packs of twenty. The price is low and is called a handling fee, because you're not actually buying the coupons. Rather, the handling fee covers the person's time and expense to clip, sort, and ship the coupons—although occasionally there's a separate shipping fee. Just go on eBay and search for coupons. If you want coupons for a specific product, type that into the search box—"Angel Soft coupons," for example. Or, if you don't care about the brand, just type in "toilet paper coupons."

The offer should state exactly what the coupon is for, how many coupons are in the pack, what the handling fee is, and the expiration date of the coupons. It will also state if the shipping is included or if you have to pay an additional fee for that. So for the toilet paper example, you want to see something like this: "Save $.50 on any two Angel Soft

Toilet Paper 4-packs or ONE 9-pack or larger. One lot of 20 Coupons. Ships for $1.50. Coupons expire 6/10/13."

Make sure it's a manufacturer's coupon for cents off, because there are some fraudulent coupons out there. If you see an offer on eBay for free product coupons, chances are they are not legitimate. Manufacturers do send out some free product coupons, but they are very few and far between; most of the ones being sold on eBay are counterfeit. I don't advocate purchasing free product coupons; I stick with the cents-off ones. Before you buy any free product coupons from eBay, check with the Coupon Information Corporation (www.couponinformationcenter.com/coupon-fraud-list.php) to see if they are on the fraudulent coupon list; you can also call the Coupon Information Center at (703) 684-5307 to get information about the validity of any coupon.

Is it really worth it to pay a handling fee for coupons? Well, if it's for a product you really want to stock up on, this can be a very good way to do it. You don't have to buy a bunch of newspapers and you get exactly the coupons you want. Let's say you are looking for Ragu spaghetti sauce. Go to eBay and type in "Ragu coupons," and it will pull up any Ragu coupons that are out there. A pack of twenty of

Clipping Services

The coupons available on eBay are usually offered by individuals. But there are also clipping services that you can pay a small handling fee and they will send you manufacturers' coupons. Some clipping services offer them in bundles and some offer them one by one. With clipping services you can select only the coupons you want.

Some clipping services take longer than others to send out your coupons, so keep that in mind. I'm a big fan of Klip2Save.com. They have awesome customer service and have very quick shipping, but there are plenty of other clipping services too. You'll find a list of some of my favorites on my blog at http://www.freetastesgood.com/?s=clipping+service.

the same coupon is usually available for between ninety-nine cents and a dollar ninety-nine.

Let's stick with the Ragu example, because that's a purchase I made recently. At my local grocery store, Ragu was on sale for one dollar. I went on eBay and found a fifty-cents-off coupon (which is pretty typical) priced at ninety-nine cents for a pack of twenty. I ordered forty coupons, for which I spent a dollar ninety-eight, shipping included. The store doubled my fifty-cent coupon to one dollar—and remember, the Ragu only cost a dollar. So I ended up with forty jars of Ragu spaghetti sauce for—well, I can't say free, because I did spend a dollar ninety-eight to get the forty coupons. But it came out to slightly less than five cents a jar. That's a huge savings! So yes, it was worth paying a dollar ninety-eight to get all those coupons—and I was able to donate all the spaghetti sauce to help forty families.

From Other Couponers

I clip all the coupons from my Sunday newspapers, even though there are some things I just don't need. Baby items like diapers and baby food are good examples; my kids are past that stage. So I swap those coupons for others I can use. You can find couponers online who are ready to swap, including on my Facebook fan page. If you have coupons you don't need, you just post "Hey, does anybody want these baby products coupons?" And then somebody else might post, "I'll trade you your baby coupons for vitamin coupons." Then you exchange addresses and you each drop your coupons in the mail. It's as simple as that!

Another thing some people do is called a coupon trading train. You get about ten people together in a group and pick one person to start. That person mails an envelope full of coupons to the second person on the list. That person goes through the coupons, picks out what she wants, and puts in all the coupons she has that she's not going to use. Then it just keeps getting sent around, person to person, exchanging coupons. Coupon trains often go from state to state, which is why it's important to limit it to manufacturers' coupons for national brands.

To be totally honest, I tried a trading train once but didn't find it very helpful. Whenever it came to me, it seemed there were no good coupons left! But some people rave about the coupon train and think it's the greatest thing, so you might want to try it and see how successful it is for you. You may love it!

I do trade with other couponers a lot. Swapping is one reason it's always beneficial to have a network of people you can reach out to.

The Coupon Database

If you're looking for a coupon for a specific product, the insert you get in the Sunday newspapers can be disappointing; there are only going to be so many coupons, and the product you want isn't always going to be there. In addition to searching the Internet sites I've mentioned, scanning blogs, shopping on eBay, and putting out requests for swaps, you can also use a coupon database.

The coupon database I like is maintained by a Web site called Deal Seeking Mom. I've also licensed their database for my blog, www.freetastes good.com. With a coupon database, all you have to do is type in the product you're looking for—such as

"Dole Fruit Crisp"—and it will show you all the coupons available in magazines, Internet printables, manufacturers' coupons, store coupons, mailers— wherever there is a coupon for Dole Fruit Crisp. Before you go to the store, you can look up every product on your shopping list and see if there are any coupons out there.

Go to http://www.freetastesgood.com/posts/ how-to-use-the-coupon-database for step-by-step instructions on how to use the database on my Web site. You will be surprised how much this will help you save additional money.

The fans who follow my blog have told me it's the greatest thing, because they don't have to search the Internet anymore for coupons. They can just go right to the database now and find that coupon, and can even print it directly from my page.

I've found that more often than not, if you simply ask for coupons, people will step up and give them to you.

They might ask for some of your coupons in return, but that's easy to do—and hey, it's not costing you any money.

When we were filming *Extreme Couponing*, Gerber Graduates baby food was on sale for one dollar and there was a fifty-five-cents-off manufacturer's coupon available as an Internet printable. On top of that, the particular store we were shopping at for the show had a special offer that runs on Thursdays, Fridays, and Saturdays, where any coupon over fifty cents automatically became a dollar. Are you getting the picture? That baby food—on sale for a dollar—was going to be free. The only question was how many coupons I'd be able to find.

First, we have three computers, so I could print six Internet printable coupons. Then I posted on my Facebook fan page "I'm looking for Gerber Graduates baby food coupons, and this is where you can find them. It's all going to be donated to charity, so would anybody be willing to get these coupons and send them to me?" I asked everyone to send the coupons to our church.

The folks at Sharp Entertainment were blown away when more than three hundred coupons came in. It was fun to open all those envelopes from California, Arizona,

Texas, Florida—all over the country. We laid them all out so you could see the postmarks from all the different states, and it was so cool to see how people stepped up and got involved. I loved being able to show how great it is to network with other people and how effective it can be.

Takeaway Tip$

Why Do I Need to Collect So Many Coupons?

Most products go on sale every eight to twelve weeks. The way to get the most value from your coupons is to buy the product with a coupon when it's on sale. So the more coupons you collect, the more items you can buy when they are on sale.

However, I've given you a lot of coupon sources in this chapter. You don't need to hit them all right away. Start with the sources

continued...

you feel comfortable with and get yourself organized. Then investigate one or two other sources of coupons and see how they work for you. Take your time and slowly expand as you get into the rhythm of couponing.

Am I Going to End Up Spending More Money Buying Newspapers Than I Will Be Saving with My Coupons?

Each week, based on the coupons you are seeing in the Sunday insert, you have to decide. Is it a better deal to buy more copies of the newspaper? (The answer is yes if you want multiples of many of the coupons in the insert.) Or is it cheaper to pay the handling fee and purchase them on eBay or from a clipping service? (The answer is yes if you want multiples of just a few coupons.) A handy Web site, www.sundaycoupon preview.com, shows all the coupons in the upcoming Sunday insert by Tuesday or Wednesday of the week before, so you can decide if you're going to want additional Sunday papers. And remember, there are plenty of ways to get more newspapers without buying them.

What If I Want a Coupon for a Specific Item?

Go to the manufacturer's Web site and see if the company offers coupons. If there isn't a specific offer, try writing to the company to say how much you like the product—it very well may send you a coupon.

There is also a coupon database on my blog, www.freetastesgood.com, where you can type in what product you are looking for and the database will tell you if there are any coupons out there and where they can be found. If they are printable coupons, you can print right from my blog.

continued . . .

What If I Want a Lot of Coupons for a Specific Item?

You can put out a request in your couponing community and offer to swap coupons for the ones you need. You can also pay a handling fee and purchase coupons from eBay or clipping services. If you shop smart, what you spend on the coupons will be tiny compared to what you save.

What's Wrong with Photocopying Coupons I've Printed Out Myself?

The bar code changes each time you print out a coupon, but not when you photocopy it. The store gets reimbursed by the manufacturer only once for each unique bar code, so by using a photocopy, you're essentially stealing the value of the coupon from the store.

CHAPTER 3

Getting

Organized

have seven children, and as you might imagine, our family has a lot of dates, activities, and appointments to keep track of. So I have a big calendar on which I mark all my kids' events, showing when we have to be here, there, and everywhere. If I didn't have a good system for keeping everything organized, there's no way I could keep track of it all.

It's the same with couponing. I have a system. Think about all those coupons you've gathered after reading chapter 2. When you go to the store, you need to know what items you have coupons for. If you have a manufacturer's coupon and a store coupon for the same product, you want to be able to combine them to maximize your savings. And coupons do expire, so you have to organize them so you remember to use them. The number-one reason people tell me they stop couponing is they can't get organized and it becomes too much of a hassle. I don't want that to happen to you!

The more organized you are, the less time you're going to spend couponing and the more savings you will enjoy. This is the most important thing to remember. It's worth it to spend a few hours getting organized right from the start, because that's how you will get the best results. In my opinion, getting organized is the most critical part of couponing.

In this chapter, I am going to tell you about my system for getting organized. But first I want to say that you don't need to follow *my* system. You just need to follow *a* system. I know everybody organizes things in different ways. Reading about my system will help you see all the things that need to be accounted for and give you some ideas about how to get started. But in the end, you need to think about how *you* want to organize your coupons and what system will work best for you.

Maybe my system will work for you just as it is, but you can always tweak it to suit your needs, or you can create a system all your own. I actually tried three different systems before I found the one that worked for me. So here's my advice: Choose a system to try, then go to the office supply store or order online whatever you need for that system, and be ready to invest some time to set it up. Use it for a month and see how it works for you. Change what doesn't work (you may have to keep tweaking different areas) until eventually you get a system that works well. Getting organized in a way that feels comfortable *for you* is what's going to encourage you to keep couponing.

My Basic System

I keep my coupons in a big binder. Inside the binder are clear plastic sheets that are made to hold baseball cards. Each sheet has nine pockets. The sheets are organized into sections by shopping category—such as dairy, frozen foods, canned goods, and skin care—and each section is separated by a plastic divider.

I went through four binders that fell apart and dozens of section dividers that ripped before I realized this is one area where buying the more expensive, high-quality supplies really does save you money in the long run. Trust me, use the heavier-duty supplies; you are going to be flipping through your binder so often that with cheaper ones you'll end up replacing the binder and dividers and even the plastic sheets every couple of months. See the box below for tips on buying binders and dividers.

Joni's Get Organized Shopping List

☐ **Binder**

I use a binder that has two separate three-ring sections—one on each side. Often, these double-sided binders will have a set of smaller rings (maybe 1.5 inch) and a set of larger rings (maybe three inch). I personally find it helpful to have two sides to my binder. I keep grocery coupons on the three-inch ring side, and all my cleaning and hygiene product coupons on the other, smaller side. A zipper runs around the whole thing and it has a little handle on top, so you can close it up and carry it like a briefcase. There are several different brands out there, ranging anywhere from ten dollars all the way up to thirty-five.

☐ **Plastic binder dividers**

I use Avery Dennison Ave-11201 Avery Style Edge Clear Plastic Insertable Dividers. They're entirely plastic—the paper ones tear and fall out too quickly. A set of eight is about seven to eight dollars. You will need two sets.

☐ **Plastic card holders**

I keep my coupons in baseball card holders. These are eight and a half by eleven inches—the same size as a standard sheet of paper. You can get them from Target, Walmart, eBay, Amazon, and hobby supply stores. They cost about six dollars for a pack of twenty-five or fourteen dollars for a hundred. Some people use plastic sheets made to hold currency, because the pockets are a little bit longer and the coupons you print off the Internet tend to fit better into those. Others like plastic sheet protectors, the kind you use for school reports, so they can insert whole sheets from a circular rather than cutting out individual

continued . . .

coupons. Get whichever plastic sheets you prefer; you can even mix it up and use a combination of currency holders, baseball card inserts, and full-page protectors. Whatever kind you purchase, go for the more expensive, heavier plastic ones that won't tear as easily.

☐ **Scissors, two pairs**

You'll want a bigger pair for cutting out coupons at home and a smaller pair that you can tuck in a pocket of your binder to take to the store with you.

☐ **Calculator**

Get something small and flat and inexpensive that you can slip into the binder and take to the store with you. You don't need to do fancy math with it; you just need to figure out when something is an awesome deal.

☐ **Accordion file**

Get a heavy-duty plastic one so it will stand up to some wear and tear. I use the C-Line 13-Pocket

Poly Expanding File, which is about five dollars. It's ten inches wide and five inches high—big enough for any coupon I've cut out. I like it because it has tabs you can write on, and it closes with an elastic band and a button. This way, the coupons I've presorted don't fall out in the car or in my shopping cart.

Filing your coupons within the binder is the most important part of getting organized. Some people do it alphabetically, and if that works for you, that's great. For me, that takes too long! Instead, I stick to general categories, which I've written on my section dividers. You'll find my list in the box on page 82. This list corresponds roughly to the way products are grouped in the aisles of a supermarket. For example, the frozen foods are always together in a couple of aisles in the store, the dairy products are always together, and so on.

Joni's List of Section Dividers

Below are the headings that work best for me. They correspond to the way supermarket aisles are laid out so I can use my binder at any store and know exactly which section my coupons are in. But again, you should use whatever system works best for you.

FREE*

Produce

Condiments

Beverages

Snacks

Candy

Baking

Breakfast

Canned goods

Packaged items

Meat

Frozen foods

Paper products

Cleaning items

Medicine

Dairy

Store coupons**

Coupon policies

Skin care and shaving

Feminine care

Oral care

Hair care

Pets

Cosmetics

Baby products

Future sale coupons***

*FREE: You're never going to find anything cheaper than free, so there's no need to save these

continued ...

coupons until the item goes on sale. I want to make sure I use them before they expire, so I put them right in the front.

**Store coupons: When an item goes on sale at a specific store, you want to be able to pull your coupons *from that store* and match them up with manufacturers' coupons for the sale items. Filing the store coupons separately helps you do that quickly.

***Future sale coupons: These are coupons I have for sales coming up in the near future. You can view Walgreens, Rite Aid, and CVS sales online two to three weeks ahead of time, and set aside your coupons for items you know will be going on sale. If you file those coupons under a separate tab by the week the items will be on sale, you won't forget to use them when they will get you the best value.

This way, when I get to the frozen food aisles, I just flip to that section in my binder. As you know, when you go down the frozen food aisles, all the ice cream is together and all the vegetables are together and all the frozen waffles and pancakes are together, so some people add another level of organization within each section. For example, within the frozen foods section of their binder, they might sort the coupons by frozen vegetables, frozen pizzas, frozen breakfast foods, ice cream, and so on. I don't do that because I think the more elaborate your organization system, the harder it is to keep it up. For me, simple really works. But, as I said, that's just me. It's all personal preference—do what works for you.

The one thing I will really recommend is that you don't organize your binder by the aisles in your local supermarket—like aisle one, aisle two, aisle three. What if you decide to go to a different store? That store's aisle one isn't going to be the same as aisle one at the store you usually shop at. But no matter what store you go to, you know it's going to have a baking aisle and a personal care aisle. So categorizing each section the way a typical supermarket is organized will make it a lot easier for you to find things, no matter where you shop.

Within each section, I arrange my coupons in the pockets by expiration date so the ones that are going to expire first are in the top pockets at the front of the section, and then I arrange them consecutively by expiration date. At the beginning of every month, I go through my binder and remove any coupons that are getting ready to expire or have expired. (But don't throw them away! I'll tell you what you can do with them in chapter 9.)

If I have a store coupon and a manufacturer's coupon for the same product, I file them side by side in their appropriate tabs so I can quickly see where I have a store coupon to match with the manufacturer's coupon.

Within each pocket, I keep the coupons in packs of ten, because most stores have a five- or ten-coupon limit— you can only buy five or ten of the same item on the same shopping trip using coupons. I'll staple each pack of ten together or put a paper clip on them so I can just pull them out ten at a time, rather than having to count them as I'm going up and down the aisles.

Two Variations on the Basic System

I know some people who don't cut out their coupons. They use the binder system, but they simply separate the pages of the Sunday inserts and put each whole sheet in a clear page protector, like the kind you might use for school projects. Then they create a cover page at the start of each section listing what coupons are inside, with the expiration date noted beside each coupon. Rather than writing a new list each week, you could also print the list of coupons from SundayCouponPreview.com (which I mentioned in chapter 2), and put that in front of each insert. Then when you are at the grocery store, you can just look at that page to see if any of the coupons you need are in the inserts you have.

Some people don't bother with a binder at all. They just use a filing cabinet or accordion file and file their inserts by date and by the company that produced them (SmartSource, RedPlum, etc.). When

continued ...

they're ready to go to the grocery store, they make a shopping list. Then they look on my coupon database to see which insert had the coupons they need, and on what date. They pull out those coupons from their filing cabinet and they're ready to go.

If you don't cut your coupons, always file them by date. So if you are using the binder inserts or just a filing system, all your copies of the January 1 insert would go together, the January 8 insert, and so on. Within the date, file them by whatever company produced the insert. This way, it's still pretty easy to pull the sheets when they have expired.

How Much Time Does It Take?

You'll need to invest some time at the start to set up your system. If you decide to just follow my binder system and see how that works for you, I'd estimate it will take you three hours at the most to get set up, because you won't have to stop to think about how to organize your coupons.

If you want to set up your own system, it will take a bit longer because you need time to work out how you want to organize your coupons, where you want to put things, and how your system will work.

But as I've already said, that's time very well spent. If you're not organized, you are going to become frustrated and you're going to stop couponing. There's nothing worse than spending your first shopping trip searching through all the coupons that you stuffed into an envelope! You're going to say, "It took me five hours to shop, and my time is money! Did I really save anything in the long run?"

Once you get your system set up, it doesn't take much time to maintain your coupon library, as long as you keep at it every week. In our house, organizing coupons is a fun family activity. Every Sunday evening we sit down with all the inserts and the Internet coupons I've printed, and we cut them all out, sort them, and put them in the binder.

I usually get ten inserts every Sunday. I tear out the same page from each one, stack them up neatly, and cut through all ten with my paper cutter (the kind with a board and a big long blade that you whack down). The kids then sort the coupons and stuff them in the pockets of my baseball card holders.

It's kind of a nice family activity for us, because we all sit around together and play coupon math. We challenge the kids with questions like "If I have a coupon for seventy-five cents and the store doubles, how much is the coupon worth?" This leads us to the next question, "If the item is on sale for a dollar ninety-nine and we have a coupon for seventy-five cents and it doubles, how much are we going to pay for the product?" (Of course, our favorites are the ones that will be *free*, because we all love *free*!) We also play coupon memory: Turn the coupons over and try to find matches. This is a very special bonding time for our family. Not only are the kids learning math skills, but they are learning how to be frugal shoppers and how important it is to give back to others. Plus, it's great to have a reason to just hang out all together.

It usually takes us about an hour to cut and sort all our coupons for the week, depending on how many games we play. If you don't have seven kids to help you out with your couponing, it might take you two hours to cut and sort everything and put it all together in your binder. The time may also vary week to week; maybe one Sunday you get only one insert and another you have five. Do it while you're watching TV and you won't even notice that the time has passed.

Two More Things to Put in Your Binder

In the front of my binder, in full plastic page protectors, I keep a copy of the coupon policy of every store I shop at. You can find these online. Go to the store's Web site; there is always a search box up at the top of the home page. Type in "coupon policy" and it will come up. Print it out and take it with you.

Why do you need these? First of all, knowing the store policies will help you decide where you want to shop. Before you started couponing, you probably never really paid attention to which store accepts what kinds of coupons or what its policies are. But once you start couponing, it's really important to know which stores double coupons or give you money back when your coupons exceed the price of the product. You want to find out which stores offer the best value for your coupons and start shopping there.

Second, you'll find that stores are always hiring new cashiers, so it's inevitable that you're going to sometimes check out with a cashier who isn't aware of the store's policy. Here's an example from a woman in my blogging community.

At Walgreens if you have a dollar-off coupon for a product that's on sale for only ninety-nine cents, the cashier has to manually enter the coupon at ninety-nine cents because the cash register won't accept a scanned coupon worth more than the price of the product. This woman went to her local Walgreens with a dollar-off coupon for a ninety-nine-cent product and the cashier told her, "We can't accept this coupon." My friend knew the cashier was wrong, but unfortunately, she didn't have a copy of the store policy with her.

You, however, are going to avoid this mistake! Just take that store policy out of your binder and show it to the cashier. But please, be extra nice about it, because most cashiers aren't trying to frustrate you. They just aren't that familiar with the store policies and they don't want to do anything wrong. Nine times out of ten, when you show them the policy you've printed out, they'll make the correction. (That tenth time, very politely ask to see the manager.) That's why it's important to have the policy with you when you go to the store.

The other thing I always have with me is an aisle-by-aisle store map for all the big stores I shop at. Usually you can get that on the store's Web site. But if you can't find it there, go to the service desk in the store and ask the staff for one. They almost always have an aisle-by-aisle map that they'll copy for you. You can use your aisle map to plan your shopping trip before you even leave home.

Organize Your Shopping in Advance

When you have the Sunday circulars and the store circulars and have looked at all the store and coupon Web sites, you'll end up with a lot of information to process! Even with your well-organized binder, you can find yourself wandering up and down the aisles, flipping pages and pulling coupons as you go, and spending a lot of time shopping.

A woman who took my couponing class told me that the first time she went couponing she was in the store for seven hours! She had no idea what was in each aisle, she had no idea what coupons she had (even though she had organized them in a binder), and she was beyond frustrated. That's why it's so important to sit down with your aisle-by-aisle store map, your coupon binder, your sales circular or the price matching from a blog for a specific store (more about that in chapter 6), and get your shopping trip organized at home.

Before I go shopping, I think about what I need and check the store circular to see what's on sale. Then I sit down with my binder and start pulling out the coupons for what I want to buy. I put the coupons in an accordion folder, arranged by aisle in the supermarket—that's why I have the aisle-by-aisle maps in my binder. I put everything I'll find in aisle one in the first pocket of the accordion folder, everything in aisle two in the second pocket, and so on.

This system works even if you're shopping in a store you've never been to before—as long as you have the aisle-by-aisle store map. Going to the store and just wandering around trying to find things and matching them up with your coupons takes up way too much time. But if you have it planned out ahead of time at home and you know what aisle every item is in, you can navigate quickly and smoothly through the store.

That accordion file ends up being kind of like my shopping list. When I hit aisle one, I pull out all the coupons I've filed under aisle one. As I pick up each item and throw it into my shopping cart, I put the corresponding coupons in the back of the accordion file facing backward (this is my way of keeping track, like crossing something off a list). If I still have coupons in my hand when I reach the end of aisle one, I know I've forgotten something.

Of course, our best-laid plans can sometimes get really messed up. When I was filming *Extreme Couponing*, they wanted a list the day before of everything I planned to buy in the supermarket. That way, they could go to the store early and plan all their camera setups and where they'd need to put the lights and so on. Well, one time, I made a spreadsheet of everything I was going to purchase, with the aisle number in the first column and the item in the second column. When I finished the list, I clicked at the top of the column to put it in alphabetical order.

The next day when we started filming, we quickly realized something had gone terribly wrong. We went down the aisle where I was supposed to be buying hot sauce, and it was nothing but pet food. Looking for detergent, I found boxes of pasta instead. I finally figured out that when I'd alphabetized my list, I had sorted only the first column on my spreadsheet; all the aisle numbers stayed where they were, but all the product names moved around. We had no idea where we were going. It was horrible!

That was probably my longest day of filming. The shortest was the one showing a competition between me and another extreme couponer. We each had thirty minutes to get all our items. I *thought* I was a fast shopper, but of course I'd never actually timed myself, so I didn't know how I'd do. I was really hustling—or running, I should say. In one aisle I had to bend down to get a box of cat litter, and I'd been going so fast that I started seeing stars and almost passed out. I had to grab the producer.

My organizing system was a big help on that superspeed shop. But I had other help too. I was allowed to bring one person with me to tell me what items to get. Jamie followed me to every aisle (he was allowed to stand at the end of each aisle) and shouted out what items to get. We already knew which side of the aisle everything was on, so with him calling out the items I was able to move superfast. I also had a lot of people there to support me—cousins, aunts, uncles, nieces, nephews, my sister, and two very good friends, Jennifer and Amy. It was supercool to have them all there cheering me on. (If you watch that episode, you'll notice there's a guy who resembles country singer George Jones browsing in every aisle I was in. That's my uncle Dale. He really wanted to be on TV, so he listened to Jamie yell what aisle I should go down, found his way there, and pretended to be shopping. He got his wish to be on television, and now he's in a book too. I *love* my uncle Dale!) In the end, I bought over two thousand dollars' worth of groceries (all donated to charity)—and I did it in less than five minutes!

Being Organized in the Store

Even though I presort my coupons into my accordion file, I always take my binder with me to the store. You never know when there's going to be an unadvertised special, and you want to be ready to maximize your savings by combining that sale price with a coupon (more about that in chapter 5!). Plus, sometimes even I forget we need something, or I won't remember to pull a certain coupon out of my binder. So all my coupons are always there in case I need them.

Any additional coupons I pull out of my binder, I put in the accordion file. That way, when I get to the checkout, I have all my coupons in one place and I know for sure that my coupons and my purchases will match up. The cashier scans the bar code on your groceries and scans the bar code on the coupons, and if something doesn't match up—say you handed her avvcoupon for a box of Hamburger Helper but you didn't buy any, or a buy-one-get-one-free coupon for a box of cat food but you only bought one box—the cash register will reject the coupon. That slows down the cashier and delays your checkout, so it's best to have the right coupons in your hand.

If you bring whole insert pages with you to the store rather than cutting your coupons at home, make sure you pull the pages out of your binder as you go through the store. With the pair of scissors you keep in your binder, cut those coupons either as you shop or while you're waiting in line at the register—although you may find yourself standing in line worrying, I hope I finish cutting before I get up to the cashier. I know you don't want to annoy the cashier or the people waiting in line behind you by holding up everything.

Take All Your Coupons with You

Let's say you're going to the supermarket for toilet paper, orange juice, and chicken pot pies. You take the coupons you have for those items from your binder, you look through the circulars to see where these items are on sale, and you go shopping. Why bother taking your whole binder with you?

Because when you get to the grocery store, you may find there are unadvertised sales that were not in the Sunday paper or the store circular. You really can't know everything that's on sale until you get to the store. Here's a perfect example: Recently I went to Walgreens, where bags of six disposable razors usually sell for $7.99. To my surprise, the razors were in the clearance bin for $3.49. Luckily, I had a three-dollar-off coupon, so I paid just forty-nine cents for a package. If I hadn't had my binder with me, I wouldn't have been able to turn this into such a sweet deal.

Because I'm so organized and so visual, I like to have my coupons already cut out so when I get to the store I can just pull out what I need. When I'm messing around with whole pages from an insert, I'm always afraid I'm going to drop some and I get all frazzled. But that's me. Some people would rather keep the pages together and cut out the coupons at the store. It's all about your personal preference. Do what works for you. Just get out there and do it!

Takeaway Tip$

Why Do I Need a System for Organizing My Coupons?

The more organized you are, the less time you're going to spend couponing and the more money you will save. If you clip out coupons and just stick them on the refrigerator with a magnet, I promise you are not going to use most of them.

They'll end up expiring and eventually you'll just take them down and throw them away. Plus, the number-one reason people tell me they stop couponing is that they can't get organized. The only way you'll stick to it is if you work out a system and prepare yourself properly.

What's the Best Way to Organize My Coupons?

I know I sound like a broken record, but seriously, do whatever feels right for you. A lot of people will try one way and find it doesn't work for them, so they'll try something else. Take the time to work through it and see what system is best for you. If you force yourself to do it my way even though you tend to organize things differently than I do, you won't want to coupon anymore. And that's the last thing I want!

continued...

How Much Time Is It Going to Take Me to Get and Stay Organized?

At the start it will take you two or three hours to get everything set up and organized. (If you're thinking through a whole new system, it may take a bit longer.) After that, if you keep up with it weekly, you should not have to invest more than an hour or two a week.

Why Do I Need to Bring a Store's Coupon Policies with Me When I Go Shopping?

Stores hire new cashiers all the time, and they are not always familiar with the store's policies. When you have the policy with you, it's easy to help the cashier figure out how to handle your coupons. Do remember, though, that store polices change frequently, so make sure you always have the most up-to-date policy.

Why Should I Bring All My Coupons with Me to the Store?

Stores have unadvertised specials and things that end up in the clearance bins. You can still use your coupons for all that merchandise—but only if you have them with you!

How Do I Get Together All the Coupons I'm Using So I Have What I Need When I Get to the Register?

Before you go to the store, put the coupons you know you'll be using in an accordion file (or an envelope, or your purse, or whatever you're using). Add any coupons you pull from your binder as you shop to the same accordion file (or envelope, etc.). Don't try to do it while you're waiting in the checkout line, because then you have to rummage through everything in your cart to remember what you bought. It's easier to pull the coupons out as you walk up and down the aisles.

CHAPTER 4

Learning the
Coupon Lingo

Let's start this chapter with a little quiz. Catalina is:

a. an island just off the coast of Southern California.

b. a type of yacht.

c. a checkout coupon you can use for money off your next purchase.

d. a company that makes swimsuits.

The answer is c. Although, to be perfectly fair, all the answers are correct. But if you're an extreme couponer, c is the one you care about. It's the coupon that prints out at the register after your transaction is complete. Usually, it's good for several dollars off your next purchase. It's called a

Catalina because that's the name of the company that creates many of these couponing programs.

Couponers are a community of people who share the mind-set that they always want to save money and get a bargain. Like any community, they have some insider language. This is the lingo couponers use when talking to other couponers about what deals they can get from different stores, inserts, and Web sites. When I first started and I was looking at other people's blogs, I saw things like "Find this coupon in the 4/15 SS," and it seemed they were speaking this crazy language—I didn't have a clue what they were talking about. With all these abbreviations and shortcuts, it was really overwhelming at first because none of it made sense. I knew they were saying significant things, but I had no idea what they meant. What in the world is SS?

It's important to know the coupon lingo so that when you are following a blog or talking to other couponers, you'll know what they're talking about. Fortunately, all the couponers use the same lingo. In this chapter, I'll fill you in on all the insider terms and acronyms extreme couponers use to talk to one another.

Catalinas

Let's start with Catalinas, since you already know what those are. A Catalina is an OYNO coupon—that's "on your next order." You use it the next time you buy something at that store. Stores with rewards programs might call Catalinas by a special name as part of their program. But no matter what they're called, they're all basically the same thing. Here are some of the most common OYNO programs.

Store	OYNO Program	Couponer Lingo
Rite Aid	+Up Rewards	Plus up or +Up
CVS	Extra Care Bucks	ECB
Walgreens	Register Rewards Balance Rewards* (*Yes, they have two!)	RR BR

In-store flyers and tags on the store shelves will usually tell you that a Catalina is available if you purchase a particular product, or spend a certain dollar amount. Local stores will usually tell you on their Web site if they're offering in-store Catalinas.

Catalinas are sometimes printed right at the bottom of

your register receipt, and sometimes they are printed separately. They tend to expire fairly soon after you get them, usually within two weeks. They also may have very specific requirements, so be sure to read them carefully. For example, they might offer a certain number of dollars off your next purchase of twenty dollars or more, or off your next purchase of a certain category such as vitamins or store-brand items, or off the purchase of one specific item. If you're lucky, they'll be for a dollar amount off anything in the store.

Too many people don't use Catalina coupons! Sometimes they don't remember to take them with them, or they throw them out when they get them, simply *assuming* they won't remember to take them. Sometimes they don't want to buy the product the Catalina is for, or they didn't want to buy the product that generates the Catalina in the first place. But I'm here to tell you: A Catalina can make money for you, even if you have to buy a product you are not going to use. You can turn it into a moneymaker by rolling your Catalina.

If you sail yachts, rolling your Catalina would be a bad thing. But for an extreme couponer, it's a great achievement. In my first episode of *Extreme Couponing*, I was able to roll my Catalinas and get over five hundred cups of yogurt for *free*, plus turn them into a moneymaker. Here's how I did it: The store was offering a seventy-five-cent Catalina with every six yogurts you bought. I had manufacturers' coupons that made the yogurt free. So for every six I purchased (which, with my coupons, cost me nothing), I got a seventy-five-cent Catalina that I used to buy other items to donate to our local food bank.

Catalina Rolling Etiquette

Remember, a Catalina is only good OYNO. Some stores will let you do several transactions at the same register to use your Catalinas, and some ask you to make your next transaction at another time. Even if the store will let you roll your Catalinas with multiple transactions at the same time, please be mindful of the people waiting in line behind you. It may be best to do one transaction, go to the end of the line, wait your turn, and then do the next one.

Here's another example. Recently a local store offered Starbucks Refreshers, the fruit drinks, for ninety-nine cents; plus, you got a ninety-nine-cent Catalina with every purchase. At the same time, there was a coupon for a *free* Starbucks Refreshers in the Sunday newspaper insert. So when you bought one Refresher using the coupon, you got it for free, *plus* a ninety-nine-cent Catalina that was good for anything in the store. If you had ten coupons and purchased ten Refreshers, you would spend nothing and receive $9.90 OYNO, which you could use to buy things like milk and eggs that you usually can't find coupons for. And if you didn't want the ten drinks, you could simply donate them to a food bank. This is why extreme couponers take their Catalinas very seriously!

Price Matching

Price matching means matching up the sale price with a coupon. This is the basic strategy for extreme savings— including getting stuff for *free*. I talked about this a little bit in chapter 3 on getting organized, and we'll go over the strategy in more detail in chapter 5.

Coupons in the Store

In chapter 2 I described all the kinds of coupons you might find in a store. But just so you have all your lingo in one place, I'll go through them again here.

- Tear pad: a coupon, typically placed near the product, that you tear off from a pad
- Blinkie: a little machine that dispenses coupons, also typically placed near the product
- Peelie: a peel-off coupon placed on a product

Stacking

Stacking means pairing a store coupon and a manufacturer's coupon for added savings on a single item. If the item is on sale, even better! (Not all stores allow you to stack, though, so be sure to check the store's coupon policy.)

Manufacturers' coupons come directly from manufacturers. You are more likely to find them in a Sunday insert or on the manufacturer's Web site or a Web site where you can print Internet coupons. It will say "Manufacturer's Coupon" right on the front.

You're likely to find a store coupon on the Web site for the store or in a store circular or flyer. It will say "Store Coupon" on it, and may also have the logo of the store. Sometimes it's a "clipless" coupon, meaning you don't have to cut it out; the coupon will automatically be applied when you scan your store savings card at the register.

Two places that come to mind where you can almost always get free or nearly free products by stacking are Walgreens and Target. The last time I bought Bayer aspirin, for example, it was on sale for $2.99 at Walgreens. I had a two-dollar-off manufacturer's coupon and a one-dollar-off coupon from Walgreens, so I put the two of them together and got that Bayer aspirin for free. At Target, Activia yogurt was on sale for $2.19 for a four-pack. I had a dollar-off manufacturer's coupon and a dollar-off Target coupon, so I got a four-pack of Activia yogurt for nineteen cents.

Make sure both coupons have the same product description and size so that they can be used together for one purchase. For example, if one coupon is good only for a two-pack and one coupon is good only for a four-pack, you can't stack them. And remember, one has to be a manufacturer's coupon and one has to be a store coupon to be able to stack. You cannot use two manufacturers' coupons or two store coupons for the same item.

Newspaper Inserts

The Sunday newspaper inserts are known by the names of the companies that produce them. You need to know this because coupon bloggers refer to them by their initials. When they're doing price matching for you, they'll give you the information about where to find the coupon in shorthand—such as SS 5/13 or 5/13 SS, which means the SmartSource insert that ran on May 13. Here's a list of insert abbreviations.

- GM = General Mills
- PG = Procter & Gamble
- RP = Red Plum
- SS = SmartSource

To find the name of the producer of a particular insert, look on the spine. That's where you will also see the date of that insert. It's in very tiny print, so you may need your reading glasses! I know I do.

Printed on the Coupon

The text printed on the coupon explains exactly how you may—and may not—use the coupon. "Manufacturer's Coupon" and "Store Coupon" are two examples we have already discussed. Here's another pair of terms you need to understand: "one per purchase" and "one per transaction." "One per purchase" means you can use the coupon to buy one item, so if you want to buy five jars of peanut butter, you need five coupons to get the discount on each.

A purchase is not a transaction, though. A transaction is one trip to the register. If a coupon says "One per transaction," it means you can use only one coupon each time you check out at the register. So with that kind of coupon, if you buy five jars of peanut putter at one time, you can use only one coupon and get one discount, while paying full price for the other four jars of peanut butter. If you have several "one per transaction" coupons, you can get around this by making multiple trips to the store that week.

A lot of people get confused about the difference between a purchase and a transaction. A purchase is one item; a transaction is one trip through the checkout line. Even the cashiers sometimes get confused. If that happens to you, pull out the store policy from your binder and explain it as nicely as you can. After all, it *is* confusing!

"Maximum value" is something you'll usually see printed on a coupon that offers an item for free. It sets a limit on how much the manufacturer is willing to reimburse the store for a product. Let's say you have a coupon for a free bag of cat litter. It says "free" in large print, but the small print usually says something like "Maximum value $6.95." So, depending on the size you choose, "free" may not really mean *free*. If the litter sells for more than $6.95, you have to pay the difference. If you truly want the litter for free, you might have to wait until it goes on sale, or shop at a different store that offers it at a lower price.

Unfortunately, there's a big market for fraudulent coupons out there, and a favorite tactic is to reproduce free product coupons without the maximum value. So if you are offered a coupon that says "free" but indicates no maximum value, it is very likely fraudulent.

Another term you might see printed on a manufacturer's coupon is "Do not double," meaning the manufacturer will only pay the store the face value of the coupon. In that case, it's up to your store whether to double or not. In fact, most stores that double coupons set up their registers to automatically double, no matter what the coupon says. They get reimbursed only for the face value of the coupon anyway, and pay for the doubling themselves—no matter what the manufacturer prints on the coupon. They've chosen to accept that as a cost of doing business. But be aware that it is up to each store not to double the coupon if it doesn't want to.

Note that if a store doubles your "Do not double" coupons, you're not doing anything illegal or wrong. That's just the store's policy. If the store chooses to offer this service to its customers, it knows what it's getting itself into. Don't worry about it!

Describing the Coupons

Couponers use abbreviations to describe exactly what a coupon offers or the various types of deals that are available with coupons. If you want to get into swapping or you buy from a clipping service, it's especially important to understand this lingo, so you know exactly what you are getting.

- MC or MQ: manufacturer's coupon
- IP: Internet printable
- EX or X: expires on
- NED: no expiration date
- DND: do not double
- DNT: do not triple
- B1G1 or BOGO: buy one, get one free
- B2G1: buy two, get one free
- FAR: free after rebate
- TMF: try me free offer
- IVC: instant value coupon; these are found in the store circular at Walgreens and are good for in-store savings, so these are store coupons

Filler

A filler is an item purchased to reach a minimum total on an order so you can get a deal. Some store policies say you need to have as many products in your transaction as you do coupons. So if you want to use three coupons, you need

Couponing as a Community Service

A lot of religious and community groups are now getting involved with couponing because it helps them stock a large number of items in their food pantry or soup kitchen. They might ask members to drop off all of their coupon inserts, and organize one group to clip coupons and another group to do the shopping. This means they have more supplies to help more families, without costing the group a whole lot of money.

I love how it lets everyone get involved at whatever level they're comfortable, whether it's just bringing in their inserts, collecting them from colleagues at work, clipping coupons, doing the price matching, or actually shopping. All are great ways to give back to your community and pass the blessing on!

to buy three items, even if all the coupons are going to be used for only one or two of them. Let's look at an example.

Suppose I have two dollar-fifty-off coupons for Tylenol. Each bottle costs four dollars, or eight dollars total. Minus my coupons, I owe five dollars. I also have a Catalina for five dollars off my next purchase. But that's three coupons for only two items, a no-no per this store's policy: three coupons only work if I have three items. So I need a filler item, something very inexpensive; maybe a can of tomato sauce for twenty-nine cents or an individual Laffy Taffy for only ten cents. I can grab one of these items as a filler and use my three coupons. Got it? Easy-peasy!

Just a Few More

As I said before, couponing lingo is a kind of shorthand communication. For example, YMMV stands for "your mileage may vary." It means the coupon may not work for you. Some offers are regional, so just because an offer will work in Toledo doesn't mean it will work in Los Angeles. On my own blog, when I'm not sure if a certain deal is regional or national, I'll write YMMV to let people know I don't have confirmation that you can use it everywhere. I just want to warn people that what looks like a great deal may not work in their area.

Here are a few more common abbreviations everyone uses.

- OOP: out of pocket, the amount you have to pay after you've used all your coupons
- GC: gift card
- MIR: mail-in rebate; you'll have to mail some kind of proof of purchase to get a rebate check
- SCR: single check rebate; some stores that offer rebates mail out rebate checks once a month; they add up all the rebates you're entitled to (usually through an online program), and once a month send you a single check for the total

All this lingo, which you'll see on my blog and many other couponing sites, is really just a way of cutting down on what we have to type. What's funny, though, is that I am actually a very talkative person! My first time filming *Extreme Couponing*, I kept talking to everyone in the store. I do that all the time because I want to share with everyone how to coupon. While we were waiting in the checkout line, for instance, I kept turning around and having conversations with the customers behind us. I talk to the cashiers too. In fact, I have a kind of catchphrase when they are about to give me my total: I always say, "What's my total after coupons, sista?"

After about an hour of this, our producer asked me to stop talking to everyone. I couldn't understand why. Later I found out it's because they had to get a signed release form from every person I talked to, in case they wanted to use that scene in the show. The production assistant actually had to run out and make extra copies of the release forms as a result of my chattiness!

Takeaway Tip$

Why Do Couponers Use All This Lingo?

It's just a kind of shorthand, a way we can all communicate with one another without having to type out the same phrases over and over. All

continued . . .

coupon bloggers use the same lingo, so you only need to learn it once. But you do need to learn it, because otherwise you won't be able to understand where and how to find the best offers.

How Can I Combine Manufacturers' Coupons and Store Coupons?

You can use one manufacturer's coupon and one store coupon for each individual item you purchase. So, for example, you could combine a CVS store coupon for Crest toothpaste with a Procter & Gamble coupon for Crest toothpaste and use both coupons to buy one tube of Crest (or maybe even get it for free!). This practice is called stacking.

However, you cannot use two manufacturers' coupons or two store coupons for the same product. So if you have two CVS coupons for Crest, you need to buy two tubes of Crest to redeem them both.

What's the Difference Between a Purchase and a Transaction?

A purchase is buying one item. So if you go to the checkout line and buy ten cans of soup, you have made ten purchases. A transaction is one trip through the checkout line. So when you go through the checkout line to buy those ten cans of soup, you have made one transaction.

What's the Difference Between a Catalina and a Register Reward and an OYNO Offer?

They're all the same thing: a store credit—a dollar amount you can use on your next transaction in that store.

How Will I Know When a Catalina Is Going to Be Available for Something?

In-store flyers and tags on the store shelves will usually tell you that a Catalina is available if

continued ...

you purchase a particular product or a certain dollar amount. Local stores will usually tell you on their Web site as well. Another Web site to check out is CouponNetwork.com. Click on "Your-Bucks" and you'll see offers that come with a Catalina in specific stores.

CHAPTER 5

How to Maximize Your Savings

P icture this: You have a coupon for seventy-five cents off a box of Cheerios. The fourteen-ounce box is $3.99, so with your coupon it will cost you $3.24. You saved seventy-five cents, which is great, and you didn't pay full retail price—which you should *never* do for breakfast cereal! If you save just seventy-five cents a day couponing, that's $273.75 a year—who wouldn't want that nice chunk of change in their pocket?

But you can do *so* much better, and in this chapter I will explain how. Some of these techniques I have already touched on in other chapters, but this is where I get into the juicy details of how it's done. I'm going to share all my secrets with you, because while a bargain tastes good, *free* tastes even better.

Wait for a Good Price Match—
Know When to Hold 'Em

When you start couponing, you may get excited and think, Wow, I'm going to save money today! You can, but not as much as if you hold on to your coupons until the item goes on sale. When I tell people about this strategy, they sometimes say, "Why wait? With that coupon I'm still saving seventy-five cents, and if I go to a store that doubles coupons, I'm saving a dollar fifty. That's pretty good!" They're right, but instead of looking at what you are saving, I always tell people to look at what you are *spending*.

In the example I started with, you could use the coupon you have to buy your box of cereal for $3.24, or $2.49 if the store doubles. But an extreme couponer will always hold on to that coupon until the cereal goes on sale, to maximize her savings. Pairing up a coupon with an item that's on sale is called price matching. When done right, waiting for a price match can net you really cheap or even *free* products.

If you save that seventy-five-cent coupon and wait until Cheerios go on sale for two dollars, you'll only spend a dollar twenty-five a box, not $3.24 (that is, instead of saving seventy-five cents, you've saved $2.74 off the full retail price). And if the store doubles coupons, the box of cereal that usually retails for $3.99 will cost you only *fifty cents!*

This is why you really need to hold on to the coupon until the item goes on sale. That's how you maximize the savings. Remember in chapter 2 I talked about the sale cycle? Most things go on sale about every twelve weeks. So just be patient and wait until the sale comes around again. Now, I know what you're thinking: You're worried that the coupon will expire. Store coupons usually do expire within a few weeks. But manufacturers' coupons are typically good for at least a month or two, if not longer. And honestly, even if your coupon does expire, it's crazy to be paying $3.24 for a box of Cheerios when you know that down the road there is going to be another coupon and another sale and you're going to be able to get the cereal for a lot less.

As you get used to price matching, you'll start to get a sense of when things are about to go on sale. My friend's husband loves Ciao Bella ice cream, which tends to be kind of expensive. She noticed that about every three months,

Ciao Bella goes on a buy-one-get-one free sale. So they stock up when it's on sale and get enough to last them for three months.

Of course, if you need something right away, go ahead and buy it. Use a coupon if you have it so at least you don't have to pay full price. But if it's not something you need urgently, do your best to wait until it goes on sale.

You need patience to wait for the perfect or almost perfect price match. And as it turns out, you also need patience to film a TV show. It takes two twelve-hour days to film a fifteen-minute segment of *Extreme Couponing,* and a lot of that time is spent standing around and waiting. One day during filming, as we were waiting for the sound guy to get everything set up, I said to Jamie, "What do you think Isaiah would be doing now?" Isaiah is my ten-year-old son who loves Michael Jackson, and he had just learned how to do the moonwalk. In answer to my question, Jamie started to moonwalk, which never fails to crack me up. It's so easy to forget that the camera is on you at all times, even when you're not talking or really doing much of anything. So when the episode aired, we were surprised to see Jamie moonwalking across the grocery store floor! In that same episode, there was a sign by the customer service desk that said "For Good Service Ring Bell." If you look closely, you'll see Jamie ringing the bell over and over. He was just bored and goofing around. We had no idea that it would wind up on the air! On TV shows that have written scripts, I'm sure the cast do much more outrageous things while they're standing around waiting. The difference is that on reality TV, it all gets filmed—and, more often than not, they end up using that footage! But that's okay; I don't mind that America sees the goofy side of me and my family. That's just who we are.

In chapter 6 I'll talk about how you can use local and national blogs to do the price matching for you. But you can also do it yourself by sitting down with the Sunday papers. The coupon inserts are there and the supermarket circulars are too, so all you have to do is match them up.

Stack Your Coupons

Stacking means pairing up a manufacturer's coupon and a store coupon to get double the savings on the same item. I talked about it in chapter 4, so I know you already have the idea. The blogs that do price matching for you will also give you information about stacking.

My very favorite kind of stacking allows you to end up with *free* products. It's simple: stack a manufacturer's buy-one-get-one-free coupon with a store's buy-one-get-one-free coupon. The manufacturer's coupon covers one item and the store coupon covers the other, so you get them both for free!

This is a case where it's super-important to know the store policy, because not all stores will allow you to stack buy-one-get-one-free coupons. If you end up with coupons like that, it's worth it to find a store that will take them both. Which leads me to my next topic. . . .

Pick Your Stores

Sometimes the store that's the cheapest when you don't have coupons is not the cheapest store when you're couponing. You probably already know which stores in your area have lower everyday prices, and shop there. But sometimes it's worthwhile to go to the more expensive stores if they have a better coupon policy.

In fact, most people, once they start couponing, end up

totally changing their shopping habits. You will start shopping at different stores because the stores you used to think were more expensive really aren't if you get more for your coupons and more free products.

Go to all the stores in your neighborhood, even if you don't typically shop at some of them, and find out their coupon policies. I bet one or two will have better coupon policies than the rest. You're still going to play the field; you don't have to shop *only* at the store with the best coupon policies. Maybe that store doesn't stock some of the things you want, or is good for items that have coupons but not for items that typically don't, such as produce and milk. Be open to all the different stores in your area and see which ones work best for you. But I will say that once you start couponing, you often end up shopping at the stores you would least expect to find yourself in.

One of my friends is a pastor's wife. She told me that before she took my couponing class, she never shopped at A&P because it was the most expensive store in her town. But now that she's couponing, she shops there all the time and is saving fifty to seventy-five percent off her grocery bill every week.

Double Your Coupons

My friend shops at A&P because the store doubles the value of her coupons. So when she shops there, a coupon for ninety-nine cents is worth a dollar ninety-eight off. Some stores allow doubling and some stores don't. If you can find stores that do, stick with them. These are the stores to shop at because you will be able to get very cheap and even free products almost all the time.

Doubling Doublespeak

Most stores that double coupons will only do so up to a point. Typically, that's coupons with a face value of up to fifty cents, although some will go as high as ninety-nine cents or a dollar. In other words, most will double any coupon worth fifty cents or less. So if you have a seventy-five-cent coupon, they won't double it; in fact, they won't even bump it up to a dollar for you. (But again, some will bump it up to a dollar. That's why it is so important to be familiar with the store policies in your area.)

Now, here's where it can get confusing: "We double up to fifty cents" and "we double up to one dollar" can actually mean the same thing. "We double up to fifty cents" usually means your fifty-cent coupon is good for a dollar off. But "we double up to one dollar" could mean one of two things. It could mean "we double coupons up to a *total* value of one dollar" (that is, we double coupons up to a face value of fifty cents off, which means you could get a maximum of one dollar off). Or it could mean "we double coupons up to a *face* value of one dollar" (that is, we double coupons up to a face value of a dollar off, which means you get a total of two dollars off).

What the store policy *says* and what it *means* varies from store to store—which is why you have to check each policy very carefully. If you don't understand something in the store policy, ask the store manager.

Note that stores that double coupons usually put a limit on how high they are willing to go. The box on page 136 has some examples of how different doubling policies affect how much you can get for the same coupons.

Take the time to look around all the stores in your area where you might possibly shop—not just the stores where you have shopped in the past, but all the stores. Many stores put signs in the window to let customers know they double coupons. But some don't, so be sure to ask. You can even call and ask over the phone, "Do you double coupons?"

It's so important to become familiar with all the different stores in your area, so you can get maximum value for your coupons. You may find that although your local store only doubles coupons up to fifty cents, that covers most of your coupons and purchases, and only when you get coupons of higher value is it worth driving a little farther to a store that doubles bigger coupons.

Always ask if the store has a maximum coupon value that it will double. You also need to know the store policy to find out if your store doubles all the time, doubles only on certain days, doubles only if you are disabled or in the military or a senior (and what "senior" means, since it varies from store to store), and so on. A store near me offers Super Doubles three times a year, where a dollar-off coupon doubles to two dollars off. By paying attention to when Super Doubles are offered at that store, I can really maximize my savings.

Let Go of Brand Loyalty

When I was growing up, my parents always used Tide detergent. I liked how it made our clothes smell. So, probably because that's what I was used to, when Jamie and I got married, that's what I always bought. But Tide is very hard to get for free—you can get it cheap, but very seldom can you get it for free. We started noticing that you can get Purex and All and some other brands of detergent for *free*, and we thought, Let's try it and see what we think. So we did. And you know what? It turns out *free* smells pretty good too! Now we're flexible about what kind of detergent we use.

A lot of times, the brands we feel loyal to are just a matter of habit or whatever we grew up with. But the more product loyal you are, the less money you are going to save. It's better to keep an open mind, try something new, and see how it works for you. Remember that in my family, we found something else that cleans our clothes and smells good— and it's *free.*

But hey, I know that old habits die hard. If you try something new and you just don't like it, well, okay, then. I'm not suggesting that you start using products you really don't like! For example, Jamie is totally loyal to Jif peanut butter. We've tried other brands and he only likes Jif. I've even tried to trick him by putting other brands in a Jif jar, but he can tell the difference. So when I can get a good deal on Jif, I really stock up. And meanwhile, with all the money we're saving couponing, we can afford to get him what he loves.

Still, in general, the more you can venture away from specific brands, the more money you are going to save.

I actually made up my own brand name while we were filming the finale of *Extreme Couponing All-Stars* in Las Vegas. A box of pasta I was carrying in the store came open, and some of the pasta fell out. When I started to say that there was something wrong with the box, what came out

Try It, You'll Like It

Sometimes you get a high-value coupon for something you don't typically use or eat. Maybe it's an ethnic food you've never tried before or a different brand of salad dressing or a new laundry product. If you can get it for free or very cheap, why not? You may find you really like it.

If you're absolutely not interested, swap the coupon with somebody else who is. Or, if the item is free, get it and donate it somewhere. Pass the blessing on.

was the made-up word *bojanky*. I don't know where it came from, but it made sense to me at the time and was fun to say! So all during filming, I referred to that as my box of bojanky pasta. We're not supposed to use brand names in the series, so the film editor wanted to know why the producer allowed me to keep referring to that "brand called Bojanky Pasta!"

(And guess what? Free "bojanky" pasta tastes pretty awesome too!)

Save Big by Thinking Small

Conventional wisdom states that the biggest package of something is the most economical. To make sure we can all compare the value of one size package to another, stores are required to display the unit price of each product—that is, how much one unit, such as an ounce, costs in the small carton versus the large carton. When you compare unit prices, it's often true that the bigger package is a better deal. But that's only when you're paying full retail price for an item. And extreme couponers *never* pay full retail price.

Believe it or not, when you have coupons, the best deal is often on the *smallest*-size product. Maybe not if all you got was one tiny little trial-size bottle. But if you could come home with a bagful, and they were all *free*, well, *that* would be a great deal! And that's exactly what you'll get if you have coupons for a dollar off *any* size of a product, which means you can get the trial size for free.

You have to read the coupon very carefully, though, because some coupons specify a particular size or a condition in parentheses, such as "excluding trial and travel sizes." But if the coupon says "on any," that includes the trial sizes, and you're good to go.

Here's an example I use in the classes I teach. Not too long ago there was a dollar-off coupon for Arm & Hammer toothpaste that had no size restriction. Several of my local stores sell the small tubes for ninety-nine cents, so with every dollar coupon I could get a free trial-size tube of toothpaste. Now, a lot of people in class say, "But the big tube is three dollars, or two dollars with the coupon, and I get ten times as much toothpaste, so how am I really saving money?" Well, I got twenty of those dollar-off coupons on eBay for ninety-nine cents, which I used for twenty trial-size tubes of toothpaste. Twenty trial sizes are the equivalent of two large tubes of toothpaste, which would have cost me four dollars (two dollars each, using the coupons). So I saved three dollars and one cent.

Sometimes you really need to sit down with your calculator and do the math, but I'd say ninety-nine percent of the time if you can get a trial size, you will be saving a ton of money. All you have to do is make sure the coupon says "any." Look right below the description of the product and it will say in parentheses whether the coupon excludes anything. It might say "excluding trial sizes" or "excluding travel size." But "any" means there are no size restrictions.

Here's another example: A while ago there was an Internet printable coupon for a dollar off any Minute Maid juice. Most people think, With a dollar off, I'm going to buy the big jug; it's the best value, so then I'll really be saving money. And it's true that the big jug is usually five dollars, so the coupon represented a nice twenty percent savings. But Minute Maid sells smaller, individual cartons of juice that usually cost ninety-nine cents each. So with the coupon, you could get one of those for free.

If you have only one coupon, there's not much difference between getting the trial size for free and getting a dollar off the larger size. But when you have multiples, your savings add up—and very quickly! Our local community center goes through a lot of juice in their kids' programs, so we asked people at our church to print off those Minute Maid coupons for us. After collecting sixty coupons, we got, *com-*

pletely free, sixty small cartons of juice—the equivalent of fifteen of the big jugs, which would have cost sixty dollars (fifteen times four dollars)!

As we discussed in chapter 2, usually you can only print two or three Internet printable coupons per computer, but there are ways to get more, so you can still save considerable money. And to me, even two or three free items are better than something you have to pay for.

Rain Checks—They're Not Just for Baseball Games

If you go to a store and they're out of stock on an advertised sale item, go to the customer service desk and ask for a rain check. This is typically just a slip of paper stating what the product is and what the sale price is, plus an expiration date—usually thirty days from the date you got your rain check. The next time you're in the store, you can purchase the product and give the cashier the rain check, and it will be rung up at the sale price.

I try not to get too worked up about it when the store is out of stock on a sale item. As I told one of my couponing classes, "With the coupon craze right now, you may find the shelves cleared very quickly."

One of the ladies in class raised her hand and told us how she carefully planned her shopping trip but the majority of items she planned to buy were sold out. So she marched herself to the customer service desk and gave everyone an earful. I smiled and asked her, "How did that work for you?" She said, "What do you mean?" And I said, "Well, you still walked out of the store with nothing, right?" There's no point in becoming irritated and irate at people. Just politely ask for a rain check. It's not the end of the world.

Sometimes these things turn out for the best anyway. On one of my shopping trips I planned to buy several boxes of cereal bars. They were on sale for ninety cents with my coupons, which was a decent price—not the best price, but decent. However, I went to the store two days in a row and it was out, so finally I got a rain check.

The next week they still weren't there, or the week after that. Two weeks later, though, they were in stock. That same week the store was giving a Catalina for two dollars off every three boxes. With my rain check and the Catalina, the cereal bars ended up costing me only nine cents a box, so the rain check became a huge blessing for me.

Of course, by the time the product is finally in stock, there may be a higher-value coupon available, so again, that's a bonus! You never know when it will work to your advantage. Most people don't want to deal with getting a rain check, but I think it's worth it, especially if it's for a product your family uses all the time.

A couple of notes about rain checks. First, most stores will not give you a rain check for an unadvertised special. The item usually has to be in the sale circular to qualify for a rain check. Also, keep track of when the rain check expires. Typically, a rain check is good for thirty days. (If the product still isn't in stock thirty days later, most stores will extend the rain check for another thirty days.)

Overage—Get Paid to Shop

When you have coupons that are worth more than the price of what you are buying, the amount left over is called overage. Some stores—by no means all—will give you that overage in cash. For example, there was a five-dollars-off manufacturer's coupon for any Similac baby formula, liquid or powder, any size—no restrictions. At the same time, Walmart was having a sale on Similac, for $3.84 a can. So with my five-dollar-coupon, there was a dollar sixteen overage. That meant for every can I bought, Walmart actually gave me a dollar sixteen in cash back. (Remember, the manufacturer reimbursed the store five dollars for each coupon, so Walmart wasn't losing any money.) With twenty coupons I bought twenty cans and donated them to our local pregnancy center. I received $23.20 in overage, with which I purchased our milk, our meat, and our produce—things you don't usually have coupons for. What a win-win!

Save Every Coupon

The Sunday inserts have plenty of coupons in them for products I don't use. Sometimes I decide to try something new, especially if I can get it for free. (I've discovered I really like a lot of foods I didn't think I would!) But even with coupons I know I'm never ever going to use, I can sometimes turn these into moneymakers.

Let me explain how this works: Recently, Walgreens had a promotion for a sleeping aid—the product cost ten dollars, and the store was offering a ten-dollar register reward (a.k.a. a Catalina) when you bought one. But a few weeks earlier, there had been a coupon in the Sunday paper for three dollars off this product. So even though I don't use sleeping aids (I have seven children and a very full schedule—I have no trouble falling asleep!), I went to the store, bought the product for seven dollars (that's the ten-dollar price minus my three-dollar coupon), and got a ten-dollar register reward. So in the end I actually earned three dollars for a product that I donated. We couponers call that a moneymaker. I used that three dollars to buy milk, which I didn't have a coupon for.

Remember, it's important to keep every coupon because sometimes it can be a moneymaker for you, even if you are not interested in the product. And then you can donate the product to someone who does need it and pass the blessing on.

Very few stores allow overage where you can actually walk away with cash in your hand. In fact, Walmart is the only national chain I know of that does. But if you find a store in your area (check that store policy!), take advantage of it, even if you wouldn't normally shop there and even if the deal is for a product you don't need. I don't have a little baby at home, but I was happy to help somebody else by buying Similac and ended up making money in the process.

Even if stores won't give you overage, with some deals you may end up with a register reward or a Catalina, and that's still a moneymaker for you. When Ecotrin was on sale for three dollars for two bottles, I used two dollar-fifty-off manufacturers' coupons that were good for any size, and got the two bottles for free. Then at the register I got a two-dollar Catalina, so it actually was a two-dollar money-maker. Even if you end up paying a dollar but getting five dollars back, you've made four dollars that you can use at that store. Just donate the items you don't need.

Takeaway Tip$

Why Is It So Important to Wait Until an Item Goes on Sale Before I Use a Coupon?

Waiting for a great price match will save you the most money by far. When you do the math, buying something on sale one time and using a coupon the next time doesn't save as much as when you combine the sale price with the coupon.

Won't My Coupon Expire While I'm Waiting?

Not likely. Manufacturers' coupons tend to be good for a couple of months, and things tend to go on sale every eight to twelve weeks. So you're eventually going to end up with a price match, when your coupon will go the extra mile for you.

Is It Better to Stick with the Stores I Have Always Shopped At?

Not when you're couponing. Rather than picking

continued...

stores that have the best everyday prices, you're going to want to go to stores that have the best coupon policies. Extreme couponers never pay full price, so the full price doesn't matter. Look especially for stores that double your coupons.

What If There Are No Stores Near Me That Double Coupons?

Think about how far away from your home you are willing to go to find a store that doubles. Then check the local couponing blogs to find the closest stores in your area that double.

If you live in a place where supermarkets don't have a lot of competition, or if you live in a crowded urban area, you may not find a store that doubles coupons. Don't worry about it! You will still save a lot of money using the other techniques in this book. I have described every technique I know. Some will work for you and some won't. Do what you can and what you feel comfortable doing. You don't have to do it all. I promise, you'll still save.

There Are Certain Brands I Just Love. Do I Have to Give Them Up to Save Money?

Not at all! Just save up coupons for those brands and wait until they go on sale. Price matching will save you plenty. My friend is a big fan of Weight Watchers cheese, which is usually four dollars a package. She had two seventy-five-cent-off coupons that she held on to for two months. Finally Weight Watchers cheese went on sale at her local supermarket, at two packages for five dollars. She bought two and used her two coupons, paying $3.50 for two packages of cheese—less than the regular price of one!

Is the Biggest Package of Something Always the Best Deal?

Not when you have coupons that say you can

continued ...

purchase any size. Often, the smaller or trial sizes are the better option—if you can get multiple coupons. Whip out your calculator and do a little figuring: How much product is in a small-size package and what will it cost you to buy it with a coupon? How much product is in a large-size package and what will it cost you to buy it with a coupon? How much will it cost you to get the extra coupons? Then calculate whether a small size is the best deal for you. Most times, it will be.

If My Local Stores Don't Give Cash Overages, Should I Bother with the Deal Anyway?

Absolutely! Cash is great, but if your overage comes in the form of a store gift card, a Catalina, a rebate check, dollars on your store savings card, money off your gas bill, or any other way— take it! It's *all* good.

CHAPTER 6

Let a Blog Do the Price Matching for You

Couponers are a community—and a very nice community, in my experience. They're willing to share what they know and what they have. Sure, you have some who are all about keeping everything for themselves and just want to see how much they can get. But, judging from the people who follow my blog, I think most are very generous. In fact, as people become aware of how generous you can be through couponing, it changes them. Every Sunday I challenge everybody in my blog community to donate five items to their local food pantry, food bank, or a family they know in need, and I hear from people all the time that they have taken up the challenge and how good it makes them feel. It truly is better to give than to receive.

On one level, it's nice to follow a couponing blog just to

be part of a community of like-minded people. We couponers definitely have a lot in common, because our mind-set is to always get a bargain. Not everyone feels that way—although I can't imagine why not! But as nice as it is to connect with fellow couponers, that's not the biggest benefit of following a blog. The real reason is that good blogs do the price matching for you, so you don't have to sit down with the store circulars and all your coupons and match up the coupon deals to what's on sale at the store.

The people who maintain these blogs get all the sales circulars and check all the company Web sites and coupon databases for you and match it all up just the way you would do it—except it might take you hours to do all that price matching, and you can get the information you need in a few minutes from a blog, saving you a ton of time.

Depending on what you're looking for, you can find blogs that offer a lot of other information as well. Everyone is blogging for different reasons, and everyone is following a blog for different reasons. Some people just want to save money for their own family; some people are looking for ways to be able to give back. Some people are interested only in grocery store blogs, while others are looking for blogs that cover a wide range of stores.

Every blog will have its own way of organizing or presenting the same information too. In chapter 3 we talked about how everyone gets organized in their own way, and that applies to blogs as well. So find a blog that gives the information you need in a format you find easy to use. You don't have to follow a dozen blogs; just find one or two that cover the stores in your area and that suit your personality, your couponing style, and what you are looking for.

I have to say, my own blog, FreeTastesGood.com, definitely reflects my personality. I am superorganized in a very visual way, but also very chatty and upbeat. I try to encourage others while still having a ton of fun interacting with everyone.

Actually, sometimes my friendliness can go to extremes! While filming our second episode of *Extreme Couponing*, I met a stocker in the store named Bob. Bob was no kid, and he was very serious. As I mentioned before, we spent all day in the store filming each episode, so I tried to get to know as many people there as possible and let them know how much we appreciated their hard work during the filming.

Well, Bob really wasn't interested in visiting with me. It seemed every aisle we went down, Bob was there, with an expression that said he was thinking, Lady, please leave me alone. But I couldn't help trying to strike up a conversation. I am also very touchy; I often don't even realize how much I'm touching people. So every time I passed Bob, I would squeeze his arm or rub his back and say, "How you doin', Bob?" He would just give me "the look" and say, "Okay."

Well, on top of my chattiness and touchiness, I'm a competitive person, as you know, and I became determined to get him to lighten up and smile at me. Finally our sound guy asked Bob if he would pose in a picture with me and Bob said, "Okay." Bob put his arm around me, and just as they snapped the picture, I planted a kiss on his cheek. In the photo, you can see Bob *just* beginning to crack a smile. From then on, Bob was my buddy! He was full of smiles and was a totally different guy. He was definitely one of my favorite people I met while filming.

Finding a Blog

I invite you all to visit my national blog at FreeTastes Good.com. Some other national blogs I like are Coupon Mom.com, iHeartWags.com, and iHeartRiteAid.com. You can also go to Google or another search engine and start poking around. Try typing in "price match" and see what you get.

To narrow the search results to blogs that do price matching for the stores in your area, type "price match A&P" or "price match Foodtown" or whatever stores matter to you. You can also look around on the home page of the blog; usually on the upper tabs or on the text box down the right side, there will be a pull-down list of all the stores that that particular blog does price matching for.

Pick a few likely candidates, then spend some time exploring all their features and see if they offer what you're looking for. Blogs have a lot of different features (more on that in a moment), and you may decide that you want to follow two or three, or some combination of local and national blogs, to get exactly what you need.

Don't just consider *what* the blog is offering; also think about the *how*. Every blogger blogs differently. Some people are very short and to the point; some are very chatty and write a whole paragraph on every coupon, where you'll find it, where you can use it, and even a little bit about the product. There's no right answer for what to look for; it's all personal preference. You may not even really know exactly what you need until you've spent a week or two following each blog, giving it a test drive, so to speak.

Some blogs lay everything out in paragraph form and some do the price matching in a kind of shorthand on big charts. Some give you just the basic information and some give you a whole lot more. Every blog is set up differently, so find the one that gives you the information in the way your brain digests it best. For example, I used to follow a blog that listed which store had an item on sale and what coupons were available that matched the sale, but never listed the final price. I found I really like to see the final price, so I needed a blog that put it all together for me. But you may not.

Also, every blogger's agenda is different. In my blog, for

instance, I only list free and really cheap products—the prices I would pay myself. Other bloggers list every deal they can find and let you decide whether they're worth it. It's totally up to you which format you prefer.

Local Versus National Blogs

We talked in chapter 5 about how you may do better shopping in unfamiliar stores once you start couponing; also, the supermarkets in your area may be small chains or independent stores rather than national chains. That's why you may want to find a local blog that points you to the best deals right in your neighborhood. To find a local blog, add your town to your Internet search, such as "price match Sandusky, Ohio." Or, if you live in a big city like New York, narrow it down even more: "price match Brooklyn," for example.

A local blog is necessary to learn about all the unadvertised specials in your local stores. My blog is national, but I also give information about the unadvertised specials in stores near my home in Ohio, which I find by actually going to the store. Since I can't go into stores in Texas or California or New Jersey, I ask my readers to send me info about unadvertised deals in their area so we can add them to the blog. But in general, a national blog is less likely to be comprehensive for every region.

Sometimes the unadvertised sales are just as good as what's in the circular, so I do recommend that you follow at least one local blog so you can snag all those unadvertised specials.

What's in a Typical Blog?

The main reason you're following a blog is for the price matching, so let's start with that. Usually the price matching will be arranged by store. Let's say you shop at Kroger. You'll see a list of what's on sale at Kroger that week, and where you can find a manufacturer's coupon that matches it, either from a Sunday newspaper insert (which will be listed in the couponer lingo I told you about in chapter 4, such as SS 6/2) or as an Internet printable coupon. If it's an Internet coupon, there will typically be a hyperlink that takes you to the site where you can print the coupon.

If there's a store coupon that you can stack with the manufacturer's coupon, it will list that as well.

Some blogs have a printable list, which means there will be a little box next to each deal listed. Put a check next to the deals you're interested in, and when you're done you can print out a list of all the items you checked. Use it as your shopping list when you go to the store, or as your reference guide to pulling all the coupons you need from your binder or files. This is a huge time-saver for most people.

Some national blogs also have a coupon database. I described those in chapter 3. Type any product into the database and it will tell you where you can get a coupon for that item.

Another feature is an explanation of how to use the tools on that particular blog. These instructions might be written out or presented as little videos. They can be very helpful if you're new to couponing.

Blogs may also have links to deals on magazines, clothing, Amazon, Groupon, surveys, and all kinds of ways to save. Some include general money-saving tips and ideas for living frugally.

What Can You Find on a Couponing Blog?

Depending on which blogs you follow, you might find all or some of these features.

✓ Price matching, also called ad matching, deal matching, and other terms

✓ What's on sale at local supermarkets, drugstores, and convenience stores

✓ A coupon database—what coupons are available for specific items

✓ What Catalinas are available

✓ A list of trusted clipping services

✓ Free deals and how you get them

✓ Daily deals

✓ Super sales for shopping in stores and online

✓ Information on how to use the tools on the blog

✓ A message board or a Facebook page where couponers can trade information and sometimes also trade coupons

✓ Online surveys that enable you to earn money
✓ Coupon swapping
✓ Deal forums

Some blogs list any deal that's out there, and some look only for the very best deals or specific types of deals. Some focus on supermarkets, some on drugstores, some on just one or two specific stores, such as Walmart. Around Christmastime a lot of the bloggers list various hot items, such as specific toys or electronic gadgets, and what stores have them at the best prices. On my blog, I ask people to tell me what they are looking for around Christmas and then I help them find the best deal out there.

Some blogs, including my own, offer a special coupon toolbar you can download. It sits at the top of your Internet browser, no matter where you are on the Web, and does a couple of things. First, any time the blogger you are following puts up a new post, you will see a little number pop up on the toolbar. You can click on the number and see the title of the post. If you want to read it, click again and the post comes up in a pop-up window. You don't even have to leave the Internet page you were on; it opens up in a new window. This is a great time-saving feature because you don't have to keep checking the blog throughout the day to see if there's anything new. You get the alerts right on the toolbar.

Second, you can print coupons right from the toolbar, another huge time-saver. Just click on the coupon you want and you're done! On my toolbar I also have links to store coupon policies and the coupon database, so it's all handy. You can even click on the database and then just click into the coupon from there, so you can bypass the blog entirely and save a lot of time.

Tricky Scenarios

Each week on my blog, I describe a scenario that might be a little bit complicated but that will yield a really great deal. I tell you what store to go to, which items are on sale, what coupons are available, what register rewards or Catalinas you are going to get back, and exactly how to roll them. I walk you through the different transactions step by step so you spend the least money out of pocket and get the most back. These scenarios involve multiple transactions, and when you're starting out, complicated deals can be really confusing.

Here's an example straight from my blog that shows how these things work—and why you need to learn all that lingo in chapter 4. (The Video Values referred to here are video coupons Rite Aid offers on its Web site. They are considered a store coupon, so you can stack them with a manufacturer's coupon.)

This week you will get $57.26 in merchandise, pay $0.20 OOP, and get back $15.99, so it is like getting paid $15.79 for everything!!

We currently have from last week $21 ($10 +Up Reward Schick, $7 +Up Reward Schick, and 2—$2 +Up Rewards Stayfree).

continued ...

Transaction #1

Buy (1) Just for Men or Touch of Gray Hair Color $5.99

Buy (2) Revlon Eyelash Curlers $3.65 each

Buy (2) Revlon Lash & Brow Groomers $4 each—Total After B1G1 Free Sale = $11.48

Buy (2) Sour Patch Kids at $1.99 each = $3.98

Buy (2) Always Radiant Infinity Maxi Pads 12–6 ct., Pantiliners 64 ct., or Tampax Radiant 16 ct. $3.99 = $7.98

Buy (1) small filler $0.25

Total: $29.68

Use (1) $2/1 printable Just For Men Printable Coupon

Use the $3/2 Revlon coupon from the 6/10 SS

Use the $2/1 coupon Revlon coupon from the June Video Values

Use the $2/1 Revlon coupon from the May Video Values

Use the $1/2 Sour Patch coupon from the 5/13 SS

Use the $0.50/1 Sour Patch coupon from the June Video Values

Use (2) $1/1 Always Radiant or Tampax Radiant coupon from the 6/3 PG

Use $10 +Up Reward Schick from last week

Use $7 +Up Reward Schick from last week

Pay $0.18 (Get a $2 +Up Reward Just For Men, submit for the Free After Mail-In Rebate offer found here, value $3.99, Get a $3 +Up Reward Revlon, get a $3 SCR Revlon, 2—$1 +Up Rewards Sour Patch, and a $2 +Up Reward Tampax)

Transaction #2

Buy 4 Maybelline Eye Shadows $3.59 each Total After B1G1 50% Off Sale = $10.77

Buy 1 small filler—$0.25

continued ...

Total: $11.02

Use (4) $1/1 Maybelline coupons from the 4/15 RP

Use 2—2+ Up Rewards Stayfree from last week

Use $3 +Up Rewards Revlon from transaction #1

Final cost: $0.02 (Get a $3 +Up Reward Maybelline)

So after all transactions:

Total OOP: $0.20

Total +Up Rewards: $15.99 (Get back $2 +Up Reward Just For Men, $3.99 MIR from Just For Men, $3 SCR Revlon, 2—$1 +Up Rewards Sour Patch, $2 +Up Reward Tampax, and a $3 +Up Reward Maybelline)

Final Cost: +$15.79

Total Retail: $57.26

Total Savings: 100% + $15.79 Moneymaker!!

Why Sign Up?

Some blogs will ask you to register, which means giving them your e-mail address and maybe a little bit of information about yourself, as well as picking a password. You'll then have to log in to access their various databases. Others (including mine) make all that information available to everyone, but offer you an opportunity to subscribe to regular e-mail newsletters.

To sign up, look for a box or button that says something like "subscribe via e-mail." Enter an e-mail address that you check frequently. The site may then send you a confirmation e-mail. Once you're confirmed, you will get an e-mail every day from that blogger, with links to any new offers posted and a brief summary of the day's blog posts, as well as links to them.

The advantage is that you don't have to check the blog every day to see what's on it; you can just look at the newsletter once a day and pick and choose what you want to view. Whatever links you click on will take you right to that page in the blog. If you decide later that you don't want the newsletter, you can always unsubscribe. At the bottom of every e-mail you get from the blog, in the fine print, there should be a link to unsubscribe.

Couponer, Beware

One thing you absolutely want to avoid is blogs that ask you to pay to sign up or subscribe. There are plenty of free blogs, and you should never have to pay for price-matching information. Bloggers deserve to get reimbursed for the time they spend gathering the information on their blog, but they certainly don't need to charge you to get that information; they can support their blogs in other ways.

One way is by accepting advertising. Advertising on blogs is like any other advertising: You choose to read it or ignore it.

Daily deals are one of the best reasons to subscribe to a blog. These are deals that are only good for the specific day they're posted and are usually online, so if you don't hear about the deal the day it's happening, you've missed it.

Some blogs have forums where you can discuss different things, or post queries like "I'm looking for these coupons. Can you swap?" If you want to be part of a couponing community where you can swap stories and coupons, you'll definitely need to register for the blog. On some, if you're not registered you can still view the discussions, but you can't participate.

Some blogs have moved those discussions to their Facebook fan page, so you'll need to be on Facebook and "like" their page to get in on the discussions. (The link to Facebook will be right on the blog, so you don't need to go searching for it.) Some bloggers use Twitter too, and Tweet different deals throughout the day. My twitter account and blog are connected, so when I list a deal it goes to both the blog and my Twitter account @freetastesgood.

You Don't Need to Do Every Deal

You could easily spend hours and hours each day following the blogs, gathering up your coupons, and driving all over town to shop because you never want to miss a great deal. Newbie couponers sometimes see a blog post for a great deal and they think, Oh my goodness, I have to leave *right now* and go get this deal.

But you don't want extreme couponing to turn into *obsessive* couponing. That same item—whatever it is—is going to be on sale again. You don't have to worry about missing a deal, because it's eventually going to be back. Toothpaste is one of those things people get excited about because it's a product you can often get for free. When people start couponing, they go out to get every toothpaste deal there is . . . and quickly end up with a hundred tubes of toothpaste! Then they realize, Gee, I probably could have waited a month or two.

I'm actually embarrassed to tell this story, but one Sunday about three years ago, we woke up and I told Jamie, "I'm not really feeling well this morning. You and the kids go ahead to church without me." I never miss church, but there was a great sale at Rite Aid.

Well, everyone headed off to church and I quickly got in the shower and then hit the local Rite Aids. I was so excited about all the stuff I actually got paid for taking out of the store that I stacked it up on the kitchen counter to play the "guessing game"—I have my family try to guess how much I paid for all the products I purchased.

When Jamie walked in the door and saw that enormous pile of stuff, he said, "I thought you weren't feeling well!" With a smile on my face, I replied, "Honey, I was miraculously healed."

Every single extreme couponer is going to have a similar moment—maybe not skipping church like I did (and I wouldn't recommend that), but there will be a deal that seems too good to miss. My advice is, don't sweat it. Even though I got two hundred and fifty dollars' worth of stuff for *free* (in fact, I actually got paid fifty dollars), when I look back, it seems crazy to me to have skipped church to go shopping! The same deal is going to come around again. It always does.

It also has become a family joke that if I am not at church, people are going to come looking for me at Rite Aid.

Takeaway Tip$

What Should I Look for in a Blog?

Look for a blog that offers price matching and other information in a way that makes sense to you. Every blogger has his or her own style, just as every couponer has his or her own needs. So just follow a blog that organizes and presents the information you want in a way that's easy for your brain to process.

How Many Blogs Should I Be Following?

Some people think they need to follow a whole bunch of blogs so they don't miss anything. But the more blogs you follow, the more time you're spending on them, and when you first start couponing, the more confusing it is. So you're better off finding two or three that you really like and sticking with those. Follow at least one national blog and one local blog. This way, you'll have the widest possible coverage but will still know about the unadvertised sales at your local stores.

Should I Bother Subscribing to the Blogs I Follow?

Definitely, being able to subscribe is a great feature. You will receive e-mails as soon as deals are posted. This helps newbie couponers stay up to date on all deals. You'll also be able to see at a glance what's in the blog that day and go right to the deal page that interests you.

Should I Worry If I Miss Out on a Deal?

Don't get frustrated if you miss a good deal. It's not important to get every single deal. There are great deals every day, and every item is going to be on sale again. The sale cycle is about eight to twelve weeks, so if you miss a sale this week,

continued . . .

it will come around again and you can snatch it up. Take baby steps and don't spend more time on couponing than you really can spare; otherwise it's easy to get overwhelmed by all the deals that are out there every day.

CHAPTER 7

Your First Shopping Trip with Coupons

Are you ready? It's time to head out the door for your first shopping trip. Your coupons are organized in your binder, you've mapped out all of the stores in your area and have their policies printed out, you've done your price matching, your shopping list is complete. Now it all comes together. Do you feel ready?

Maybe you do. Or maybe there's so much to do and remember that you're almost afraid to leave the house. No worries, my friend. Take a deep breath, and above all, keep this in mind: Whatever amount you save by couponing, you're doing something wonderful for you and your family. You are saving money. Period.

If you're a fan of *Extreme Couponing*, you've watched me save ninety-nine to a hundred percent off my grocery bill, so maybe you think you need to save ninety-nine to a hundred percent. But I have been at this a while and have a lot of experience. Most people who coupon don't save ninety-nine to a hundred percent all the time—although they certainly can some of the time!

Any savings you get with your coupons is better than no savings at all. So it really doesn't matter how large or how small—just remember, any amount of savings is a success. Even if you're new to couponing and you spend fifty for sixty dollars' worth of products, celebrate! That's ten dollars in your pocket. You might think, Oh, it's just ten dollars. But when you multiply that over fifty-two weeks, you've pocketed five hundred and twenty dollars.

If you go to the store and spend sixty dollars as usual but end up with a lot more products in your grocery cart, that's exciting too. So start looking at the big picture and congratulate yourself for saving, no matter the amount.

Couponing Within Your Comfort Zone

There's no law that says you have to go all out on your first shopping trip. If you get overwhelmed easily, pick out a few items to buy with coupons. Some people get overloaded just thinking about price matching and shopping for twenty or thirty items with coupons. That's okay. Focus on just two or three items your first time out. It's better to save a little than not save at all. Don't think, This was a failure because I had twenty coupons but I used only three of them. Flip the script: You succeeded because you saved money on three items!

Remember, when you start couponing you're shopping differently than you did before, and most people need a month or two to really get used to it and fine-tune their system. Don't push yourself to do things you don't feel ready for. That's just setting yourself up for failure. You already know what feels right for you. If you try to push yourself beyond your comfort zone, I can almost guarantee couponing is not going to work for you.

So give yourself time to find your rhythm, and take baby steps until you do. If fifteen coupons seem like too much to handle, take just five; if five seem like too much, take just one coupon that you know you have a price match for and see how great it makes you feel to pay so much less for one thing. With that one item, you saved some money and you learned something. Each time you do it, you'll feel more and more comfortable. It's *all* good.

And don't forget, give yourself a good, healthy block of time to get everything done. If you're rushing to pick up the kids from school or shopping on a lunch break, your mind won't be a hundred percent there. Take. Your. Time.

Try Two Trips

When you're just starting out, you might find it easier to make two shopping trips, one with coupons and one without. I'm the sort of person who can only do one thing at a time, especially when I'm learning a new skill. If you're like me, you might want to go out couponing one day and buy the other things you don't have coupons for another day. You won't get so overwhelmed trying to keep the coupon and noncoupon items straight.

Besides, two trips might mean more savings for you anyway, since, as we've discussed, you may end up couponing at a higher-priced store. You'll go to the store that has the best coupon policies for your coupon shopping. Then, for items like milk, produce and bread, for which it's rare to get a coupon, you'll go to the store with the lowest regular prices. Do whatever it takes to make it successful for you.

The very first time my daughter Lara and I went couponing, our plan was to go through the store once, buy all the products we had coupons for, put them in the car, then go back in and do the rest of our shopping. I learn in a very hands-on way, and I needed to be able to completely focus on the couponing that first time.

Well, on that shopping trip we bought about three hundred dollars' worth of stuff and paid just twenty dollars. I was so excited that I couldn't even go back into the store to buy the other things we needed! I had to get home and show Jamie how much I'd bought for only twenty dollars. That's when the "guessing game" started. I lined up all the products on the kitchen counter and told Jamie and the kids what the full retail price was, then asked them to guess how much I actually paid for everything. (Yes, they are tired of this game, to say the least—which is why I get so excited when I teach my coupon classes; everyone there is delighted to play my guessing game!)

Know Your Days of the Week

A successful and drama-free extreme couponing shopping trip starts at home with good planning. Begin with the blogs you picked out. They'll have the price match-ups one or two days before the sale starts. For example, if sales in your local supermarket start on Thursday, you can usually get those price matches on Tuesday or Wednesday.

Sales in both supermarkets and drugstores typically last one week. That means you have seven days to gather up all the coupons you'll need and get to the store. However, the day of the week the sale starts varies from store to store. So while one store in your neighborhood might run its sales from Friday through the next Thursday, another will run them from Monday through Sunday, and so on.

This information will be printed at the top or the bottom of the store's sale circular. Stores almost never change their sale days (I've been couponing five years, and none of my local stores have changed their sale days in all that time), so you only need to gather this information once. It's a good idea to note it on the same sheet of paper where you have the store policies.

I think most couponers tend to go to a store at the beginning of the sale because they're excited and don't want to miss out on a deal. Others like to go at the end of a sale on the theory that the shelves will have been restocked and they can get the items without fighting the crowds. Personally, I like to go several times throughout the week if the sale is good enough!

So find out when your stores begin their sales and get into a shopping rhythm: You might decide to hit Kroger on Mondays and Giant Eagle on Thursdays, and so on.

Of course, if your store doubles coupons only on certain days, you want to go when they double. You also want to plan your trip based on when your store restocks its shelves. Some items, such as milk and meat, are probably restocked every day. But grocery items may be restocked two or three times a week, and health and beauty products only once or twice during the sale. When items are on sale, especially the free items, they tend to sell out quickly, so you want to get there when the store is most likely to have your items in stock. Yes, you can always get a rain check, but especially when you're a new couponer I want you to be able to experience that wonderful feeling of coming home with bags and bags of groceries for so much less money, and even possibly playing the guessing game with your family. (Just remember, after a few times they'll get tired of that game, so you may have to recruit new couponing friends!)

If you're shopping at a store you're familiar with, you may already know when your store restocks—you may see the clerks out in the aisles working, or notice that the shelves seem to be fullest at a certain time of day. If you don't know, just go to the customer service desk and ask when the store restocks. If it's every day, ask whether it's in the morning or afternoon. Then plan your shopping trip accordingly.

Make Your List and Check It Twice

Now make a list of what coupons you are going to use for the shopping trip. If there's an item you really want to stock up on (I'll show you how to decide about that in chapter 8), start gathering extra coupons using the techniques I outlined in chapter 2.

Gather up your coupons and organize them according to the system you are using. This is where I use my accordion folder, as described in chapter 3. It works for me because I know what I'm going to get, I organize my coupons by store aisle, and I save tons of time in the store by planning my trip at home. But remember, use whatever organizational system works for you.

Now that you're couponing, you will be shopping at stores that are the most coupon-friendly, which means you may be shopping at stores you're not entirely familiar with. So pull out your copy of the store's layout, the rain check policy, and the coupon policy. Use the layout map to organize your coupons by store aisle for the shopping trip. Use the store policy to plan how many coupons you can use and in what combinations. This advance planning will enable you to spend the least amount of time in the store while still getting all the products you intend to buy.

As I mentioned in chapter 3, I use my accordion file instead of a shopping list. But when I was just starting out, I made a spreadsheet listing the items I wanted to buy, the quantity (based on how many coupons I had and the

Your At-Home Checklist

☐ Go to the price matching blogs you follow and make your shopping list based on the match-ups.

☐ Gather up the coupons you plan to use on your shopping trip.

☐ Review the store policy so you know how many coupons you can use and in what combinations.

☐ Know which aisle your items are in and organize your coupons accordingly.

☐ Pick a shopping day based on:

- The weekly sale days for your store
- The days your store doubles coupons
- The days and times your store restocks the shelves (know if they stock all items or if health and beauty items are stocked on a different day)

store policy), and what aisle each item was in. I sorted the spreadsheet by aisle so I could get all the items in aisle one, then all the items in aisle two, and so on. If you're a visual person, this might be a great way for you to organize your first couponing excursions.

The last thing you need to do to get ready for the big day is gather up everything you'll be taking with you to the store. I've made a checklist for you on page 194. Be sure to take your binder, even if you've already sorted your coupons and put them in an accordion folder. You want to be ready in case you find any unadvertised specials.

I have a nice big Thirty-One organizing tote that holds both my binder and my accordion folder, so I know I have everything in one place. If I'm taking a shopping list, I tuck it into the tote the night before my shopping trip, so when it's time, I can just pick up the bag and go.

Your Take-with-You Checklist

☐ The store's coupon and rain check policies

☐ An aisle-by-aisle store map

☐ Your coupon binder

☐ Your calculator and scissors

☐ The coupons you have selected in advance

☐ Your accordion folder, or whatever you're using to organize your coupons and set them aside in the store

☐ Your shopping list

Up and Down the Aisles

Once you've done all that organizing at home, your trip up and down the aisles will be a breeze. Have your list out, and your accordion file too (or however you have decided to organize your coupons in the store). Pull out all your coupons for aisle one, and start shopping!

As you put each item in your cart, double-check the coupon to make sure you've picked up the right brand, variety, and size. If your coupon is for the Charmin toilet paper four-pack and you pick up an eight-pack, the coupon will not work. Also check that the price match is really a match. For example, my store had Ken's salad dressing on sale recently for one dollar for the eight-ounce bottle. I had a dollar-off coupon, so I thought I would be getting the dressing for free. Fortunately, I double-checked and realized that the manufacturer's coupon was only for the sixteen-ounce bottle. My coupon wasn't a match that week, so I just tucked it away for another time.

Most of the price-matching blogs specify the size restriction on sale, to make sure the coupon they match it with has the same size restriction. So you should be pulling the right coupons at home. But still, when you are in the store, it's a good idea to quickly double-check.

When you toss the item in your cart, check it off your spreadsheet or shopping list. (It feels so great to cross things off a list, doesn't it?) Then set aside your coupons for that item. I flip my coupons over and put them in the back of the accordion folder facing backward so I know I have those items and am going to use those coupons. Then, when I check out, all I have to do is grab that stack from the back of the folder and hand them to the cashier.

As you're going up and down the aisles, keep an eye out for unadvertised specials. These are usually marked with shelf tags of a different color. If you have coupons for those items, pull them from your binder and put them with the other coupons you plan to use on this shopping trip.

Feel free to organize things in your cart, or not. One of Jamie's pet peeves is a messy shopping cart. He likes to neatly organize everything by size and shape so he can maximize his cart space. He especially likes to keep all the frozen items together so they stay cold. He's known as the "cart packing master." Where I would have a cart overflowing with stuff, he could pack that same cart and still have plenty of room to put more items in. He had a terrible time during filming, because I just threw stuff into his cart. We were being taped, so there wasn't much he could say about it. It looked great on camera, but it drove Jamie crazy! If you ever see us in the store, I am the lady with the messy cart walking next to the guy with the neatest cart ever.

Get Your Rain Checks

If you find that anything you planned to pick up is out of stock, make a note of it on your shopping list and put those coupons back in your binder or somewhere else where you're sure they won't get mixed in with the coupons you'll be redeeming on this shopping trip. (I stick mine in another pocket in my accordion folder.) Then head over to the service desk to ask for a rain check.

As I mentioned in chapter 5, you can get a rain check when something is advertised to be on sale but the store is out of stock. Some stores allow the cashiers to give out rain checks, but most require you to go to the service desk. Yes, you usually have to wait in line. But rain checks are worth it.

If you do find items out of stock, please remember that the person at the customer service desk is not at fault! Nobody is trying to make things difficult for you, and stores are happy to give you a rain check. So please, *always choose to be kind.*

At the end of your fabulously well-organized shopping trip, you will know exactly what items you need rain checks for. So just go up to the desk with your list ready. When I get a rain check, I put it in my binder with the coupon it pairs with, so everything is neatly organized when I return to the store to get those items.

If you want to buy multiples of the same item, you don't need multiple rain checks. For example, if you want to buy five boxes of Rice-A-Roni, you don't need five rain checks. But most stores will limit the number of items you can get with one rain check (that information will be in the store policy), and they will write the number on your rain check.

However, if the store is out of several different items, you'll need a rain check for each one. So if you planned to buy Bumble Bee tuna, Jif peanut butter, and Edy's frozen fruit bars, and the store is out of stock on all three items, you'll need three rain checks—one for each item.

Feeling a Little Nervous?

Okay, it's time to head for the checkout line. Are you a little nervous? On every episode I filmed of *Extreme Couponing*, I felt anxious too—even though I know how to coupon and have been doing it for years. I still worried that something might go wrong.

You can relax, though. There's no camera following you around. If you drop all your coupons or match the wrong product up with a coupon or forget to bring a coupon with you or need to spend minutes searching through your binder for it, it's not going to be broadcast on television.

Remember in chapter 1 I told you about Jamie's first shopping trip as a couponer? As laid-back as he is, he was sweating and red-faced as he waited to check out! Even though you know you're not doing anything wrong and couponing definitely works, you're remembering the saying that if something seems too good to be true, it probably is. You may be thinking, How can I put a hundred dollars' worth of groceries in my cart and pay only ten dollars? It just doesn't seem possible.

But it does work and it is possible.

Still nervous? Don't worry. When you see that you

continued . . .

really can do it, you'll become more and more confident each time. Meanwhile, think about this: What's
the worst thing that can happen? Let's say you've
pulled the coupon for Philadelphia cream cheese and
it turns you don't have Philadelphia cream cheese
in your cart, or you picked up the wrong size, or
you handed the cashier five coupons but you bought
only four packages of cream cheese. The cashier will
scan the coupon and the register won't accept it. So
you take the coupon back and you say, "Okay,
sorry."

That's it.

Nobody comes and drags you off to jail. The
store manager doesn't ban you from the store forever. The shoppers around you don't start pointing
and laughing. You just take your coupon back and
use it another day. And meanwhile, you still saved a
whole bundle with all your other coupons. Good for
you!

Time to Check Out

Now it's time to reap the rewards of all the work you've done. But first, if the person behind you has only a few items, let him or her go ahead of you. If you have a lot of coupons, it's obviously going to take you longer to check out. I think we always need to be more sensitive and more kind to the people behind us, especially if it's clear they'll be done in just a minute or two. Likewise, if the person behind you is disabled or elderly or has young children who are at the very limit of their ability to be well behaved in the supermarket (and even more so if they're already past that point), just let him or her go ahead of you. It's the courteous thing to do.

I stand right in front of the screen by the cash register, where each item and its price pops up as the cashier scans the item. I don't use a spreadsheet anymore, but when I started couponing, I had it right there with me so I knew what the sale price should be (now I find I can just remember). That way, I can make sure the price is correct.

If the item does not scan at the right price, simply point

it out. It may be helpful to pick up a sale circular while you're waiting in line so you can point out to the cashier what the sale price should be. But please, be pleasant about it. It's not the cashier's fault. The cashier just swipes the item across a bar code reader, and the store's computer reads and displays the price. This is not the person who programmed the computer! So many people get really upset with the cashier if things don't ring up right, but that's not helping the situation at all. It's so much easier to just politely say, "Oops, it's on sale for this price." It will be taken care of, so there's no need to get angry about it.

Please be patient as the cashier verifies the correct price and enters it manually. People who work in retail are often under a lot of scrutiny. If they ring up an incorrect price or give out credits they are not supposed to, they can lose their job. So relax . . . and treat the cashier the way you would like to be treated.

When I was in the *Extreme Couponing All-Stars Finale* in Las Vegas, our cashier, Flora, was so sweet. After we got our balance down to zero, my daughter Ciera and I were so excited that we started cheering. The producer told Flora to tell us not to be too excited yet because we still didn't know how the others had done and we might not have won. But Flora thought that sounded mean, and had a hard time telling us to simmer down. She tried about ten times and just couldn't do it. At last she got it right, but then quickly added, "But I hope you two win." How sweet is that?

After the cashier has scanned all your purchases, it's time for the coupons. Hand over all the coupons for the same product in one batch. So, for example, if I have coupons for five cans of Progresso soup, I'll hand the cashier those five coupons together. This way, I can make sure all five coupons get scanned. Then I'll hand over all the coupons for the next item. It doesn't really matter in what order you give them to the cashier—just keep all the same coupons for the same item together so you can check that they all ring through.

Now, what happens if you hand the cashier ten coupons and only nine ring up? It's not the end of the world and you don't have to be nasty about it. Just say nicely, "I handed you ten coupons, but if you look, there are only nine showing up." Where I shop, the cashiers will usually lay those coupons out and count them, then say, "Yup, you did have ten," and ring the tenth one through. You can see how handing the coupons to the cashiers in same-item batches makes it a lot easier for them to catch a mistake as well.

Share What You Have

You're ready to hit the stores. You are prepared and confident and about to save a ton of money. That's great. But I have one more thing I'd like you to do. On your first shopping trip, I challenge you to pick up five items to donate to a food bank or somewhere else they're needed. Try to get into the habit of doing it every time you go couponing—plan your five items right in your shopping list. I promise, it will make you feel so good!

You have more than groceries in your shopping cart that you can share; you also have knowledge. People in line with you are going to notice that you have ten jars of spaghetti sauce and ten bottles of detergent and ten bags of dog food and they're going to ask you about it. Use that as an opening to share what you know. Tell them how couponing is a great way to save money, and share some quick tips. Point them toward a blog you like so they can get more information.

The other thing you have to share is a binder full of coupons. I love everybody, but there is something about older people—grandmas and grandpas—that I love even more. Many older people are on a fixed income, and you can see them in the store struggling to figure out how much they can afford to buy. If I happen to glance in their cart and see some things that I know I have coupons for, I always stop, give them the coupons, and explain how they work. No one has ever taken offense, and most people are appreciative that I took the time to help them save money.

If I planned to buy ten of an item and I gave away one coupon and can buy only nine, so what? That little bit of generosity can go a long way. You never know when someone is struggling to afford their medicine or to put gas in the car. A few dollars saved could make all the difference. And if it doesn't, does it really matter at the end of the day? You know you did something kind and you helped someone out. To me, that's what really matters.

Takeaway Tip$

- - - - - - - - - - - - - - - - - - -

How Much Should I Aim to Save on My First Shopping Trip?

As much as you feel comfortable with. It takes most people a few months to really get the hang of couponing. If you get overwhelmed easily, maybe pick up just a few items using coupons. It's better to take baby steps than to jump in with both feet and get frustrated and quit couponing after a couple of weeks.

How Far in Advance Should I Plan My Shopping List?

Most blogs will post the store's price match-ups one or two days in advance, so if you need to order from a clipping service or swap coupons, you'll have time before the sale ends. The sale itself lasts seven days. Make sure you know which day of the week the sales end where you shop.

When I'm in the Store, How Do I Know Which Coupons I've Used?

As you pick up each item and toss it in your shopping cart, cross it off your list and then take the coupons and move them to another folder or envelope or pocket so you have all the coupons you want to redeem in the same place. This way, you'll have exactly what you need when you get to the checkout.

What Should I Do with My Rain Checks So I Don't Forget I Have Them?

Put those rain checks together with the coupons you have for that item, and then put them back in your binder. If you arrange the coupons in your binder by expiration date, file them by the expiration date of the rain check. If not, note the expiration date of the rain check (usually thirty days) in some other way that works for you.

continued . . .

What Happens If Some of My Items Don't Ring up at the Sale Price?

In your absolutely nicest voice, just point it out to the cashier. It helps to have the sale circular with you, so the cashier can verify the sale price. Then please be patient while he or she voids the sale and puts in the correct price. Remember, the cashier does not program the cash register and is not responsible for the error. So please, be kind to your cashier.

Should I Give the Cashier My Coupons in Any Particular Order?

It doesn't matter what order they're in. But it is very helpful to hand the coupons to the cashier in same-item bunches—all the coupons for Crest toothpaste, then all the coupons for Ronzoni pasta, and so on. This makes it a lot easier for both of you to check that all your coupons ring through.

What Happens If I Use the Wrong Coupons or Make Some Other Mistake at the Checkout?

Nothing! The cashier just hands you back your coupon, and maybe you end up paying full price for an item. Or you can put the item back. It's not the end of the world.

CHAPTER 8

Think BIG:
The Stockpile

Y ou've seen a lot of different couponers on *Extreme Couponing*, but one thing we all have in common is a stockpile. Stockpiling means buying large quantities of an item—way more than you need for a week or even a month—when you can get it at a great price. This is one of the keys to extreme couponing: thinking long-term.

As I've already mentioned, price matching is the other key to extreme couponing. You don't want to buy some items when they're on sale and some items with coupons—you want to buy everything when it's on sale *and* you have a coupon. If it's on sale but you don't have a coupon, wait. If you have a coupon but it's not on sale, wait. That's the secret to the greatest savings. But that's only possible if you have a stockpile. When you don't have a price match and you need the item, you're not out of luck—you just get it from your stockpile.

I hear you thinking, But I'm really not saving money because I'm spending money to stockpile. Well, yes, you are spending money, but you're saving way more than you spend. Let's say that with a good sale, you pay fifty cents for a box of breakfast cereal that would normally cost four dollars. You just saved three and a half dollars on one box of cereal. But if you know you eat one box of cereal a week and you buy enough boxes to last six months, you'll save your family ninety-one dollars. If you get that cereal for free (which is not hard to do), you'll save one hundred and four dollars. And that's on just one product.

Now imagine stockpiling six products you use regularly. Your savings over six months could be six hundred dollars or more. It's so important to look at the long-term savings rather than just a typical week of shopping; this is the difference between extreme couponing and regular couponing. Most people buy groceries for the coming week, or just whenever they need something. But an extreme couponer looks beyond one week or two and says, "This is a great sale; by getting six months' worth for free or supercheap, I'm *re-*

ally saving money." Yes, initially you have to lay out that money. But when you add up your savings over three months, six months, or a whole year, the number will be *huge*.

Obviously, there are things you can't stockpile, like lettuce or fresh milk. But you're going to use toilet paper every day for the rest of your life, right? And toilet paper won't go bad. Ever. If you find a great deal on toilet paper, stock up. If you don't stockpile it, when the day comes that you run out of toilet paper, it's probably not going to be on sale—and you'll have to pay full price for something that you could have bought for much less.

You've Got to Spend to Save

To get your stockpile started, you have to be prepared to spend some money to save a lot more. I know this makes a lot of people nervous, because it feels like you're gambling. So let me tell you right up front that in the first eight weeks, as you build your stockpile, you should not expect to see huge savings. But after about eight weeks, when your supply starts to grow, your spending on groceries, personal care products, and cleaning supplies will decrease by fifty to seventy-five percent. Then, as you keep couponing and stockpiling, your savings will become even more noticeable.

Let's do the math. Say toilet paper is usually sixty cents a roll, but with couponing you can get it for fifteen cents. Depending on the size of your family, let's say you use two rolls a week (now, remember, I have nine people in my family, so we use a lot more than that!). At sixty cents a roll, you're spending $62.40 on toilet paper in one year. At fifteen cents a roll, it's only $15.60 a year. By stockpiling toilet paper, you're spending $15.60 today but saving $46.80 for the year. Remember, that's just one product. Now consider all the products you use every day or every week, multiply that, and you can see how significant the savings will become.

What if you simply don't have a lot of money and can't start making a big stockpile? Just build up a supply in one area and use the savings to stockpile in another area, and then use those savings to stockpile in yet another area, and on and on from there. It's really an awesome cycle!

Go back and look at the budget you made in chapter 1. It will help you see which spending category would be the best to start stockpiling. Let's say your budget shows that you're spending more than you thought on cleaning supplies. That's a good place to start. You'll find that with extreme couponing, a little money goes a long way. If in the past you spent a hundred dollars a month for cleaning products, I bet with couponing you'll find you're spending twenty. (Or less—if you keep your eyes open, you may be able to get a lot of the things you need for free.)

Here's how the stockpiling system works: You go ahead and spend that hundred dollars—you've been spending that much anyway. Except now, with couponing, you're getting enough cleaning supplies to last six months rather than one month. So when next month comes along, you don't have to spend any money at all on cleaning supplies; just take what you need from your stockpile. That means you can take the hundred dollars you would have spent on cleaning supplies and use it to start stockpiling something else.

You Never Know . . .

I recommend you create a stockpile that will take care of your family for at least three to six months. Does that sound like overkill? Really, it's not.

continued . . .

Yes, almost every sale comes around again in eight to twelve weeks, so you can see how handy it is to have a stockpile of at least twelve weeks. But you should also have a cushion. You don't know what your situation will be twelve weeks from now. Bad things happen to very nice people all the time, from job loss to health crises to accidents to disasters like tornadoes and fires and floods. It's easy to think, when we're not struggling at this moment, that things will always be this way. My family was like that too. Then, when the economy went downhill, Jamie lost his job; we never even saw it coming.

If you think you don't need a stockpile, ask yourself, what if a tragedy hits our family? What if one of us can't work? What if one of us passes away? Are we financially secure without that income?

I never want to see you in the situation I found myself in as a single mother, having to choose between feeding my family and buying tampons. Several people have written to me that when they faced a sudden tragedy, their stockpile is what saved them. One woman told me about how her husband suddenly got sick and then lost his job. She had been couponing and building her stockpile mostly for the fun of it. But after their misfortunes, she was so thankful she'd done it, because without that stockpile they wouldn't have been able to survive. It was three months before they were able to get state assistance, and in the meantime, with no money coming in, they lived off their stockpile.

I pray nothing like this ever happens to you. But it's better to be prepared for a tragedy than to wait for it to happen.

Don't be afraid to spend the money to start stockpiling. It works. I promise! Start out small and prove it to yourself. You'll be amazed. Do it in just one area. Maybe start with toothpaste and toothbrushes, deodorant, or shampoo—these are products that can all be had for free if you pick them up at the right time. When you get these things for free or really cheap, you'll see how much money becomes available for other things, so you can start stockpiling in a different area.

Let me give you an example from *Extreme Couponing*. In one of my episodes, I had a three-dollar-off coupon for a box of cat food. I took it to a store where the cat food was on sale for $2.99, so that means it was totally *free*. Of course, I didn't have just one coupon, I had 432—that's right, I got 432 boxes of cat food. (No, I didn't clear the shelves; I preordered it—see the box on page 223.) I gave it to a local animal shelter, but if I had been keeping what I bought for myself, that would have been more than a year's worth of cat food for *free*. Then I could take all the money I'd budgeted to feed my cat and use it to stock up on something else. Pretty sweet, huh?

Plan Your Stockpile

When you're first building your stockpile, focus on the items you really need and use. Start by looking around your house and take notice of the things you use most often. Some things are obvious: toothpaste, toilet paper, soap, shampoo, dish detergent, laundry detergent, paper towels, cleaners. Think about packaged foods too: pasta, breakfast cereal, sauces in jars, beans, tea bags, bottled salad dressing, rice, canned tuna fish.

It's important to have a plan, because otherwise you may find yourself building supplies of things you don't really need. Before you stock up on an item, ask yourself: How much am I really saving? What's going to be the shelf life? Do I really use this? Just because it's free doesn't mean you should put it in your stockpile. If something is free, absolutely pick it up and donate it. But if it's something you're not going to use, why put it in your stockpile?

When I first started couponing, I very quickly ended up with about two hundred tubes of toothpaste because every time I could get it for free, I had to run out and grab it. Then, after a few weeks, I realized it would take us seventeen years to use up two hundred tubes of toothpaste! Obviously, the answer was to donate most of them. I knew I had plenty and I knew it would go on sale again anyway.

When you're planning your stockpile and making a list of the things you always need to buy, also write down each item's shelf life. For example, a can of corn has a shelf life of about two years, a can of cat food keeps for about a year, while a box of breakfast cereal has a shelf life of about six to eight months and a roll of toilet paper lasts forever. Then sort and arrange your list into groups: items for which you want a three-month supply, a six-month supply, a one-year supply, and a forever supply.

We have at least a year's stockpile for all our cleaning and personal care supplies. It saves me lots of trips to the store, and allows me to wait for the very best deal before I buy more (more about that in a moment). For example, I recently stocked up on 128 bottles of Purex laundry detergent. It was on sale for two dollars a bottle, and I had a dollar-off coupon. The sale was during a week that our supermarket did Super Doublers, doubling those high-value coupons they don't ordinarily double. So with my dollar coupon doubled to two, I got the detergent for free. I had to preorder to get that many bottles—and it took me several trips that week to stay within the store's coupon policy, but it made good sense. Laundry detergent is good for a year, so why not get it when it's free? If I'd stockpiled just three months' worth, I'd be stuck buying more three months from now, whether or not I could get it supercheap or free. And with a family as big as mine, I know that laundry detergent will be used up, no problem!

Preordering

Because you're following a price-matching blog, you'll know a few days in advance when sales are coming around that scream "stock up." If you plan to get more than ten of something, you really should preorder. Think of how frustrating it is to go into a store to get your deals, only to find empty shelves. Remember, you're not the only couponer out there. Be kind to your fellow couponers; don't be a shelf-clearer.

Most stores will ask you to come in to place a preorder in person. Ask for the manager, tell him or her that you know the item is going to be on sale and you plan to stock up. Then just tell them how many of each item you would like to preorder. After you've placed several preorders and they know you really will come in and buy the items and are using

continued . . .

coupons ethically, you can usually preorder by phone—just ask politely. And, of course, if you preorder something, you *must* buy it. That's only fair.

Some stores have a policy not to take preorders, and in that case there's not much you can do. But supermarkets have huge central warehouses where they keep all the groceries and then ship them out to individual stores. So usually it's no problem for them to just ship a little bit extra for you.

Stock Up Slowly

It should take three to six months to build your stockpile. You might be tempted to do it quicker, but you won't save as much. For example, tuna fish has a shelf life of about two years, so it's definitely worth stocking up. Where I live, the price fluctuates a lot from week to week; you can find it at anywhere from a dollar nine (full price) to fifty cents to ten cents to free. Some people see it on sale for fifty cents and think, That's half price; I'll stock up now. But I know it can go lower. So if you want to pick up a few cans for fifty cents, that's okay, but it's not the time to stock up. Sure, you're going to save with that fifty-cent tuna, but you can save a lot more if you're patient and wait to build your stockpile when tuna is ten cents, or free. Just think it through, because otherwise you are going to spend more than you have to. Of course, you will never find anything cheaper than *free*, so that's *always* a time to stock up.

When you're planning your stockpile, jot down next to each item what you think is the best price you can find it for. Remember, just because something is on sale doesn't mean it's a stock-up price. For example, twenty-five cents is what I call my stock-up price for a can of beans. When it hits twenty-five cents, I get a whole bunch of coupons and stock up on beans. When it's higher, I just wait (and eat beans from my stockpile).

You'll find my stock-up price list starting on page 226. In the column on the left, items are arranged by category, such as canned goods, breakfast foods, and health care items. In the middle column is the highest price I think you should ever pay for this item when you're couponing. In the column on the right is a good stock-up price. Even if you don't think these prices are realistic where you live (I know some parts of the country are more expensive), this will give you a starting point. Look around, check out deals, and decide what you think is the absolute rock-bottom price you can get; use that as a guide for when it's time to stock up.

Stock-up Price List		
	Highest price	Stock-up Price
Refrigerator		
Butter, 4 sticks	$0.75/box	$0.50/box
Butter, spreadable	$0.75/container	$0.50/container
Cheese, shredded or block, 8 oz.	$1.50/package	$0.75/package
Cheese, slices, 16 pack	$0.75/package	$0.50/package
Cheese, string, 8 pack	$1.50/package	$0.75/package
Cheese, cream, 8 oz.	$0.75/package	$0.50/package
Coffee creamer, 1 pint	$0.99 each	$0.60 each
Deli meat, ham, turkey, etc.	$2.99/lb	$2.50/lb.
Juice, carton	$1.50/carton	$1.00/carton
Lunchables, with drink or fruit	$1.00/each	$0.50/each
Rolls, crescent/sweet, 6-pack	$0.60/each	$0.40/each
Sour cream, 8 oz.	$1.25/each	$0.75/each
Yogurt, individual cups	$0.25/each	$0.20/each
Yogurt, 2- or 4-pack	$1.00/each	$0.50/each

Stock-up Price List

	Highest price	Stock-up Price
Freezer		
Bagelfuls/toaster strudels	$1.00/box	$0.75/box
Breakfast meals, individual	$1.00/box	$0.75/box
French fries/hash browns	$1.25/bag	$1.00/bag
Frozen dinners	$1.00 each	$0.75 each
Hot/Lean Pockets, 2	$1.25/box	$1.00/box
Ice cream, 1 quart	$1.99/carton	$1.50/carton
Juice, concentrate	$1.00/can	$0.75/can
Pancakes/waffles	$1.25/package	$0.75/package
Pizza, whole	$2.50/each	$2.00/each
Pizza rolls, 15	$0.75/box	$0.50/box
Vegetables, bagged	$0.75/bag	$0.50/bag
Meat		
Bacon	$2.00/package	$1.00/package
Beef, ground	$2.09/lb.	$1.99/lb.
Chicken breast, bone in	$1.19/lb.	$0.99/lb.
Chicken breast, boneless/skinless	$1.99/lb.	$1.69/lb.
Chicken thighs/drumsticks	$0.89/lb	$0.69 lb.
Hot dogs	$0.75/package	$0.50/package

continued . . .

Stock-up Price List		
	Highest price	Stock-up Price
Pork chops, boneless	$1.50/lb.	$1.25/lb.
Roast, chuck	$2.29/lb.	$1.99/lb.
Sausage	$1.99/lb.	$1.49/lb.
Steak	$3.99/lb.	$3.99/lb.
Tuna fish, canned	$0.35/can	FREE
Tuna fish, pouches	$0.50/pouch	$0.25/pouch
Side Dishes, Pasta, Rice		
Hamburger Helper	$0.60/box	$0.40/box
Hormel ready-made meals	$1.00/package	$0.75/package
Macaroni & cheese	$1.00/package	$0.50/package
Pasta, dried	$0.50/box	$0.25/box
Potatoes, boxed	$0.50/box	$0.25/box
Rice mixes	$0.50/box	$0.25/box
Rice, white/brown	$0.75/package	$0.25/package
Stuffing mix	$0.50/box	$0.25/box
Canned Goods		
Beans, canned	$0.50/can	$0.25/can
Broth, can	$0.50/can	$0.25/can
Broth, container	$0.75/container	$0.50/container
Chili, ready-to-serve	$0.75/can	$0.40/can
Cream soups	$0.40/can	$0.25/can
Mandarin oranges	$0.50/can	$0.25/can

Stock-up Price List

	Highest price	Stock-up Price
Peaches/pears	$1.00/can	$0.50/can
Pineapple	$0.60/can	$0.50/can
Soups, Healthy Choice, etc.	$0.60/can	$0.50/can
Soups, boxed	$0.40/box	$0.20/box
Tomatoes, canned	$0.50/can	$0.40/can
Vegetables	$0.50/can	$0.25/can
Breakfast		
Cereal	$1.00/box	$0.75/box
Cereal bars	$1.00/box	$0.75/box
Kashi/organic cereal	$1.50/box	$1.00/box
Oatmeal	$1.00/container	$0.50/container
Pancake mix	$1.00/box	$0.75/box
PopTarts or similar, 6-pack	$1.00/box	$0.75/box
Syrup	$1.00/bottle	$0.75/bottle
Snacks		
Applesauce, individual	$0.75/each	$0.50/each
Candy bars	$0.25/each	$0.15/each
Candy, bagged	$1.00/bag	$0.50/bag
Chips, Pringles, etc.	$0.80/container	$0.50/container
Crackers, Cheez-It, Ritz, etc.	$1.00/box	$0.60/box

continued . . .

Stock-up Price List		
	Highest price	Stock-up Price
Cookies, Keebler, Oreos, etc.	$1.00/package	$0.75 package
Energy bars	$0.50/each	$0.25/each
Fruit cups, 4-pack	$1.00/each	$0.50/each
Fruit Crisps, 2-pack	$0.75/each	$0.50/each
Fruit snacks	$0.75/box	$0.50/box
Granola bars	$1.00/box	$0.75/box
Gum	$0.35/pack	$0.20/pack
Popcorn, microwave	$0.50/box	$0.25/box
Potato chips, Boulder, Kettle's, etc.	$1.00/bag	$0.50/bag
Potato chips, Pringles or bags	$0.75/bag or container	$0.50/bag or container
Pretzels	$1.00/bag	$0.75/bag
Pudding snacks, 4-pack	$0.75/package	$0.50/package
Condiments, Sauces		
A-1 sauce	$1.25/bottle	$0.75/bottle
BBQ sauce	$0.25/bottle	FREE
Hot sauce	$0.50/bottle	$0.20/bottle
Jelly	$1.00/jar	$0.75/jar
Ketchup	$0.75/bottle	$0.25/bottle
Mayonnaise	$1.00/jar	$0.75/jar
Mustard, yellow	$0.50/bottle	$0.20/bottle

Stock-up Price List		
	Highest price	Stock-up Price
Peanut butter	$1.50/jar	$0.75/jar
Pickles	$1.00/jar	$0.75/jar
Relish	$0.50/jar	$0.25/jar
Salad dressing, bottle	$0.75/bottle	$0.25/bottle
Salad dressing, jar	$1.00/jar	$0.75/jar
Salsa, jar	$1.00/jar	$0.50/jar
Soy sauce	$0.75/bottle	$0.25/bottle
Spaghetti sauce	$0.75/jar	$0.50/jar
Baking		
Brownie mixes	$0.50/each	$0.25 each
Cake mix	$0.50/each	$0.25/each
Chocolate chips	$1.00/bag	$0.75/bag
Cooking spray	$1.00/bottle	$0.50/bottle
Evaporated milk	$0.40/can	$0.25/can
Frosting	$0.50/can	$0.25/can
Jell-O gelatin	$0.25/box	$0.15/box
Muffin mix	$0.50/package	$0.25/package
Oil, canola, 48 oz.	$1.25/bottle	$1.00/bottle
Oil, olive, 16 oz.	$3.25/bottle	$2.75/bottle
Pudding, instant	$0.35/box	$0.20/box

continued . . .

Stock-up Price List		
	Highest price	Stock-up Price
Drinks		
Juice, 64 oz.	$1.25/each	$0.75/each
Juice box, 8–10 oz.	$1.00/box	$0.65/box
Soda, 2 liter	$0.50/each	$0.25/each
Sport drinks	$0.50/bottle	$0.25/bottle
Silk soy milk, half gallon	$1.50/carton	$0.75/carton
Tea bags	$1.00/box	$0.50/box
Water	$0.40/bottle	$0.25/bottle
Baby Products		
Baby food, jars	$0.27/jar	$0.20/jar
Diapers, name brand	$0.17/diaper	$0.13/diaper
Wipes	$0.75/tub	$0.50/tub
Paper Products, Wraps		
Aluminum foil	$0.75/each	$0.50/each
Napkins	$1.00/package	$0.50/package
Paper plates	$1.00/package	$0.50/package
Paper towels	$0.50/roll	$0.25/roll
Toilet paper	$0.35/roll (Scott)	$0.20/roll
Plastic containers, 2-pack	$1.00/package	$0.75/package
Plastic wrap	$1.00/box	$0.75/box
Tissues	$0.50/box	$0.40/box
Wax paper	$1.00/box	$0.75/box
Ziploc bags	$0.75/box	$0.50/box

Stock-up Price List		
	Highest price	Stock-up Price
Cleaning Products		
All-purpose sprays	$0.75/bottle	$0.50/bottle
Bathroom cleaner/spray	$0.75/bottle	$0.50/bottle
Dishwasher tablets	$1.00/box	$0.50/box
Disinfecting wipes	$1.00/canister	$0.50/canister
Furniture cleaner, wood	$1.25/can	$1.00/can
Glass cleaner	$0.75/bottle	$0.50/bottle
Liquid dish soap	$0.75/bottle	$0.25/bottle
Sponges	$0.50/each	$0.25/each
Toilet bowl cleaner	$0.75/bottle	$0.50/bottle
Laundry Products		
Bleach	$1.30/bottle	$0.75/bottle
Detergent, 32+ loads	$1.50/bottle	$0.99/bottle
Dryer sheets	$0.75/box	$0.50/box
Fabric softener	$1.50/bottle	$0.75/bottle
Stain pretreater	$1.00/bottle	$0.50/bottle
Health Care		
Bandages	$0.75/box	$0.50/box
First aid travel kits	$0.50/each	$0.25/each
Ointment	$1.00/tube	$0.75/tube

continued . . .

Stock-up Price List		
	Highest price	Stock-up Price
Pain relievers	$1.00/bottle	$0.50/bottle
Oral Care		
Floss	$0.25/each	FREE
Mouthwash	$1.00/bottle	$0.75/bottle
Toothpaste	$0.25/tube	FREE
Toothbrush	$0.25/each	FREE
Skin Care, Bath		
Body lotion	$0.75/bottle	$0.50/bottle
Facial pads/wash	$2.00/each	$1.25/each
Men's body wash	$1.25/each	$0.75/bottle
Soap, bar	$0.25/each bar	$0.15/each bar
Soap, hand	$0.50/each	$0.25/each
Women's body wash	$1.25/each	$0.75/each
Hair Care		
Conditioner	$0.99/bottle	$0.50/each
Hair color	$1.75/box	$1.25/box
Hair spray	$1.25/bottle	$0.75/bottle
Shampoo	$0.99/bottle	$0.50/bottle
Stylers	$1.00/each	$0.50/each

Stock-up Price List		
	Highest price	Stock-up Price
Hygienic, Shaving		
Deodorant	$0.75/each	$0.25/each
Razor, disposable	$1.00/package	$0.50/package
Razor, high-quality	$1.99/each	$1.00/each
Sanitary pads	$0.50/package	$0.25/package
Shaving cream/gel	$0.65/can	$0.25/can
Tampons	$1.25/box	$0.50/box
Cosmetics		
Beauty tools	$1.00/each	$0.50/each
Eye shadow	$1.00/each	$0.50/each
Eyeliner	$1.00/each	$0.75/each
Foundation	$4.00/bottle	$2.50/bottle
Lipstick	$1.50/each	$0.75/each
Mascara	$1.25/each	$0.75/each
Nail polish	$0.50/each	$0.20/each
Powder, loose	$2.50/each	$1.50/each

Organizing Your Stockpile

If you stick ten cans of soup on the shelf on top of the coat closet and ten more under the bed and another ten cans in the bathroom closet, you won't be able to keep track of what you have. So when you're planning your stockpile, you also need a plan for where to put things.

If you have the space, it's a good idea to put it all in one place. If not, spread your stockpile out around your house or apartment in whatever way works for you. But you do want to have some rhyme or reason to how you store your stockpile, so at least keep all your soups together, all your breakfast cereals together, and so on. If you've really got things spread all over the house, you may even want to make a little map of where you keep everything. This way you'll know exactly where each item is. They have to be accessible so you'll know at a glance when you're running low on something and need to stock up again.

As you add to the stockpile, make sure you are bringing the older items to the front and putting the newer items to the back. If you push the old items back and add new items to the front of the shelves, the products in the back might expire before you get around to using them. So always make sure to rotate the items in your stockpile.

We keep our stockpile in the garage on heavy-duty open wire shelves. Some people have very expensive setups; some people have very inexpensive ones. It really doesn't matter. Do what works for you! If you want to get a special shelving unit, however big or small, just make sure it's heavy-duty, to stand up to multiple heavy items like laundry detergent, jars of sauce, and canned goods.

Because we have lots of space in our garage, I got myself a Peg-Board for smaller items. It's a big board with a lot of holes in it, and little pegs sticking where we hang razors, dental floss, toothbrushes, and the like—things that come in a package with a hole punched at the top. It makes it much easier to see these smaller items than if they were on a shelf. Plus, it's just like shopping at the store! It's such a simple thing, but I really love it.

When we first set it up, I'd go out to the garage and just stand there and look at it; I'd even call the kids out to join me. They thought it was hysterical. I don't think my family understands why I think the Peg-Board is so cute. But it's my favorite thing in my whole stockpile and it is *very* cute!

Location Matters

Our garage is insulated, so nothing freezes in the winter, it doesn't leak, and we don't have any problems with nibbling critters. This is a perfect spot for our open pantry. But when you're looking at your own garage, attic, or basement, you need to think about a few things.

If an area of your home gets very cold in the winter, certain things in your stockpile will freeze. That's not going to affect your canned or paper goods, but things in glass containers will freeze solid and the glass will break. Liquid soaps and detergents also can be ruined if they are frozen. And, of course, if you go to your stockpile for a bottle of dish detergent and it's frozen solid, you can't use it.

If your attic or basement gets superhot, that won't work either. Some of the things in your stockpile, such as juices and canned goods, will spoil if they get above a certain temperature.

The Stockpile Squeeze

What if you have a small place and don't have a lot of room for stockpiling? Look around your home and find a few different places to store things. Be creative. Maybe that means putting storage boxes under the bed, or storing stuff in your extra shower stall or in closets. Some people I know who live in New York City (where apartments are pretty small and everything is expensive) told me they use half their dresser drawers to do some of their stockpiling. Do whatever works for you. It's so important to find space for that stockpile, because when items are cheap to free, you'll want to stock up on them.

If your basement or garage tends to be damp or leaky, that might be okay for things you store in plastic bottles, but cans are going to rust and anything in boxes or bags will eventually be ruined. Paper products may get waterlogged too.

Plastic, glass, and cans will keep nibbling critters away, but anything in boxes or bags—even paper goods—will not be safe. Critters include not just mice but also squirrels, ants, and anything that creeps and eats. If you know you have mice or bugs anywhere in the house, that is not the place to stockpile most of your items. If a mouse or bug has gotten into a package, even just a little corner, do not use that item. It's no longer safe. Just throw the package away and move your stockpile.

Don't undermine your stockpile by storing items where conditions aren't right. It's better to put some things in the garage and some things in the attic and some in the spare bedroom.

Stockpiling Meat

When I was growing up, we went grocery shopping every week. That's how most of us do it. Now that you know about stockpiling, you know that for some things, you should be shopping only a few times a year, when you can get the absolute rock-bottom price. For things like milk, bread, and

Consider Getting a Freezer

Several years ago some friends of ours gave us a commercial freezer. They knew we had a big family, so when they shut down the Dairy Queen they owned, they gave the freezer to us. Before I started couponing, we usually kept just a few things in it, because we didn't really stockpile anything. But now that freezer is full from top to bottom.

Once you start stockpiling in a freezer, it will pay for itself in about a month's time. You'll save fifty percent on your meat bill, and then there are vegetables, pizza, waffles, ravioli, pot pies, dinner entrees, fruit, juice, and of course ice cream.

If you have a small home, get a small freezer. If your budget is really tight, get a secondhand freezer. It's always going to be a smart investment.

fresh produce, of course, you may still find yourself shopping once a week.

But what about meat? Week to week, meat may be the most expensive thing in your shopping cart. It does go on sale, though. Let's say this week ground beef is fifty percent off. You might buy enough for a meal or two; then next week when you want to make hamburgers you have to pay full price again. But what if, when ground beef goes on sale, you buy what you think your family is going to use for an entire month? You just cut your meat bill by at least fifty percent.

When meat goes on sale, it's typically a really good sale—fifty percent or seventy-five percent off, or buy one, get one free, especially on packaged meats like hot dogs and sausage. There's a seasonal aspect to meat sales that you can plan for too. Around the Fourth of July, hot dogs go on sale; around St. Patrick's Day it's corned beef; around Easter it's lamb and ham; around Thanksgiving it's turkeys; around Christmas it's ham again. And the deals can be even better when the holidays are over. All are opportunities to stock up. Check the sell-by dates, wrap the meat up well, and put it in the freezer (see the box on page 243 for tips on freezing meat).

Tips for Freezing Meat

I do a little Deals of the Week spot every other Monday on one of our local TV stations. Just before Easter last year, I was talking about freezing chicken, and the anchorman said he didn't know that meat could be frozen. I was amazed not everyone knew that! In fact, properly wrapped meat will keep in the freezer for about a year.

The first thing to do is divide the meat into meal-size portions. Depending on your family, that might be half a chicken or a whole one, or even just two drumsticks. You might cut that slab of ribs into four portions or two. Shape your ground beef into hamburger-size balls. Even if you have a big family, put aside a couple of individual servings too, such as one chicken breast or one hamburger or one pork chop, so you can pull something out of the freezer for a solo lunch or dinner.

Now carefully wrap up each portion. Use some-

continued ...

thing thick and strong, such as freezer paper (which is what I prefer) or heavy-duty aluminum foil. If you're freezing individual servings, you can put them in plastic sandwich bags with a zip top. Wrap each portion very carefully, so every inch of the meat is covered. After you have each portion wrapped, put it in zip-top freezer bags. Make sure you're using *freezer* bags—they cost a little more, but they're heavier, so they protect your meat better and are well worth it.

You can put several portions of the same thing in one freezer bag, but don't overstuff the bag; make sure it will close easily. Before you close it up, write down what's in the bag and the date on a piece of paper and slip it right into the bag facing out, so you can read it when you're rummaging through the freezer a month later. Close the bag three-quarters of the way, squeeze all the air out of it, and then seal it up and pop it in the freezer.

Now you know exactly what you have and when it went into the freezer. If it is well portioned, you'll never have to take out a frozen five-pound slab of ground beef and hack away at it on the kitchen counter.

Meat should always have a sell-by date on the package. That's not the date by which the meat spoils—it's the date by which the store must sell it. The meat is actually good for another day or two past the sell-by date. A lot of stores mark their meat down as much as ninety percent when the sell-by date is one or two days away, to be certain they won't have to throw it away. When you see a great deal like that, grab it! Just remember two things: First, when you buy meat that's close to the sell-by date, you should wrap it up and get it in the freezer the same day you buy it. Second, you must use it the same day you take it out of the freezer and thaw it. For ninety percent savings, that's not too much to ask!

Meat is also often available at lower prices in bulk packages or what is sometimes called family packs. There's a lot of meat in one package, and if you were shopping for the week it might be way too much. But since you're stockpiling and freezing it, bulk buys can be very good deals.

Specialty meat markets tend to be a little more expensive than supermarkets. But they can offer great deals if you know when to shop. Most smaller meat markets are closed on big holidays like Thanksgiving, so the day before is the best time to shop there. An hour or two before they close, most of their meat is going to be slashed between seventy-five and eighty-five percent. There's nothing wrong with the meat—they just need to get rid of it because they are going to be closed the next day and it's not going to be fresh anymore. So you're doing them a favor and getting a great deal at the same time. It's another great way to stock up on meat at a very discounted price.

Start by getting as much meat as you think you need for a month. It will probably take you a couple of months to determine what your family actually uses, but by the third month of experimenting, you'll know how much to buy, and you'll know the sale cycle in your local stores and when the meat will be on sale again.

Be sure to rotate your meat stockpile—move the older

items to the front of the freezer and put the newer items on the bottom or in the back. When you need a particular item, such as chicken drumsticks, check the date you froze it and use the older packages first.

Eating Your Stockpile

Once you've built up your stockpile, to save the most money you really should be planning your meals around what you have. So, for example, if you have a lot of pasta and jars of sauce, have Italian food once or twice a week. If you just bought a couple of pounds of ground beef, plan on making hamburgers, meat loaf, and spaghetti and meatballs. Or plan an afternoon to make a large batch of spaghetti sauce— add ground beef and other ingredients to your jarred or canned sauce, portion the sauce out into freezer bags, and your spaghetti nights will be a snap!

Of course, you'll want to add fresh produce and dairy products to your meals, but remember to shop first in your stockpile.

In our first episode of *Extreme Couponing*, our two oldest children were filmed "going shopping" out of our stockpile in the garage. My kids are usually out there looking for snacks, but I always ask them to grab some toilet paper while they're at it. Toilet paper is one of those things I stock up in forever quantities, and I got a lot of comments about the masses of toilet paper visible in this episode! The other funny thing is that a neighborhood dog wandered into the garage and ended up making his debut on national TV. Everyone thought it was our dog, and he must have thought so too, because he would not leave!

Takeaway Tip$

Why Is Stockpiling So Important?

Stockpiling is important because if you can get the item for free or very cheap and then stockpile it, you never have to pay full retail price for it again. When the item is not on sale, you can just get it from your stockpile. Every time you use an item from your stockpile instead of buying it, you free up the money you would have spent on that item.

I Don't Understand How Spending So Much Money on My Stockpile Will Save Me Money.

You need to think long-term. The really awesome deals—when things are free or at their absolute rock-bottom price—come around only once every three months or so. If you buy enough for six months at rock-bottom prices, you'll always save more. Suppose laundry detergent in your area is four dollars at full price, two dollars on sale, and one dollar when you can get a great price-matching deal. If you use twenty-four bottles of detergent a year, that's ninety-six dollars at full price, forty-eight on sale, and twenty-four when you're couponing and have a price match. It's a much better deal to buy a year's worth for twenty-four dollars than to buy a month's worth and risk having to pay full price the next time you need detergent.

continued ...

How Long Before My Stockpile Really Starts to Save Me Money?

It will take about two months before you get everything in place and start to notice the savings. In the meantime, you *will* see that you are getting probably twice as much while spending about the same amount of money. And within two months, anybody who is couponing is going to decrease what they spend on grocery, hygiene products, and cleaning supplies by fifty to seventy-five percent. Then, as you keep couponing and stockpiling, your savings will multiply!

How Long Should I Take to Build My Stockpile?

It should take three to six months to build your stockpile. You may be tempted to do it faster than that, but you'll end up spending more than you have to. Be patient and wait for the absolute best prices—that's what will get you the most savings.

What If I Don't Have Extra Money to Build My Stockpile?

You don't need to spend any more than you're already spending. Use your couponing skills to stock up on just one item each week for which you can get an awesome deal. Then the next week, use the money you would have spent on that item to stock up on something else. Keep it going and soon you'll have your stockpile without spending a penny more than you normally would.

How Much Should I Keep in My Stockpile?

It depends on how long each item will last. I advise stockpiling at least six months' worth of just about everything you use regularly. But when you find a great deal, go for nine or twelve months—if the item has the shelf life. Never stock up more than you can use before an item expires. So, for example, canned dog food lasts

continued . . .

about a year—don't stockpile an eighteen-month supply. Think about what you use in a typical month and multiply that by however many months the item lasts, and you'll know how much to stockpile.

Can I Stockpile Meat?

You sure can! Buy meat in bulk packages and when it's on sale. If you properly wrap and store your meat, it will keep about a year in the freezer. Be sure to freeze it in family-size portions so you can defrost just what you need for a meal.

Where Is the Best Place to Keep My Stockpile?

It depends on your home. Keep your stockpile where conditions are right in terms of temperature, humidity, and food safety. Keep the same items together so you can easily see what you have, and be sure to rotate your stockpile so you're using up the older items first.

CHAPTER 9

Changing the World, One Coupon at a Time

believe we are too wealthy a country for anyone to go without the necessities—especially when we have the power of coupons. Now that you know how to get things for free or really cheap, I challenge you to step up and make a difference in your community. It's perfectly okay to use your new talent to stock up for your family and friends, but it's also important to share that blessing with others. The power of couponing gives us endless ways to do that!

In just five episodes of *Extreme Couponing*, I used coupons to get twenty-four thousand dollars' worth of products, every last one of which was donated. We gave to many different organizations, from local food banks to national programs to an AIDS center at a Las Vegas church. Additionally, through the open pantry I keep stockpiled in my garage and the local charities we support, my family donates about a hundred thousand dollars a year's worth of food and other items. And remember, Jamie is still out of work and we have seven children.

Granted, I'm an extreme couponer and an overachiever, and I'm not asking you to match that. But I am asking you to donate five items each week to someone who needs them more than you do. If you're following a price-matching blog, you are finding free or really cheap items. Donating five of them is not going to break your budget, and this small act can make a huge difference in your community.

Donating Without Breaking the Bank

When you coupon, you are saving so much money that even if you're not rich, you can help others. My followers on my blog and on my Facebook fan page e-mail me all the time to tell me how much they enjoy the fact that couponing enables them to donate to others without overextending themselves financially.

One woman e-mailed to say that her family was

in the habit of donating to local charities, but their budget has been getting tight now that they've had a second child and she is out on maternity leave. With couponing, though, they can continue donating at the same level, or even more.

Another woman told me that she didn't need to coupon to get by, but she's on a fixed income and enjoys the flexibility the extra savings gives her. It also enables her to donate more items to her church food pantry.

These are just two of the many, many e-mails I get from my very generous community of couponers.

We Can't Do It Alone

I teach couponing classes around the country, and the price of admission is always to bring five items to donate to the charity of the host's choice. I know it doesn't sound like a lot, but I've taught classes that were as big as two hundred people. That added up to more than a thousand items that filled two eight-foot-long tables almost five levels high. Everyone in the class took a step back to look at it all, and I said, "You may not have thought your five items mattered, but now look at what we've done. It ends up being huge when everybody joins together."

I remember on one of the episodes of *Extreme Couponing*, we found a store that would triple the first two coupons and honor the next eight at face value, which meant we were about to score free pasta, free spaghetti sauce, free feminine care products, free hot sauce, free salsa, and a few other free items. We were partnering with Feeding America, a hunger relief charity with a network of food banks.

Remember that by the store's policy, I could use ten coupons for each item and Jamie could use ten coupons for each item, but that wasn't nearly enough. So my friends Danielle, Amy, and Megan came along to help. We started calling them the "Coupontourage." They stood at the entrance of the store and handed everyone who came in two to ten coupons for each item. We had the items ready to go in carts up front and explained to each customer what we were doing. Because the tripled coupons made the items free, all they had to do was go through the checkout using the coupons.

(We, of course, preordered all the items so there was still enough on the shelves for other customers.)

Thanks to my Coupontourage, that shopping trip yielded eight hundred and fifty pounds of food worth thirty-eight hundred dollars to Feeding America, which was equivalent to 664 meals—totally amazing! Plus, *all* the items were *free*. The coolest thing was that everyone in the store, and everyone from Sharp Entertainment and TLC too, saw firsthand how Jamie and I couldn't do it alone. We needed everyone to help. This is what is most important to me—the ability to work together to make a real difference in our communities. None of us can help everyone, but all of us can help someone. And when we do, lives are changed. It's that simple.

You'd Be Surprised Who Needs Help

If you've never known someone who uses a food assistance card or goes to a food bank, you might think everyone who needs help is a desperate character—perhaps drug addicts or people who could work but won't. But very often those who need help are working people who just aren't making enough to pay for everything they need. The way times are right now, there are lots of people who are employed but still have a hard time supporting their families.

Recently the wife of the associate pastor at a local church called me. Their son had accidentally left the freezer door open, so everything inside had spoiled. They had already used up their food assistance for the month and they had nothing to eat for the next week. She asked if it would be okay to come over to our house to use our open pantry. She was too embarrassed to go to the local food bank, where everyone knows her. Of course, our open pantry is set up so that nobody sees you come and go—you just take what you need—and I was really glad I could help her out.

Older people who are on a fixed income often need help as well. About six months ago, I spotted an older couple one aisle over from me at the supermarket checkout, and I could tell from the way the wife was going through her purse and looking upset that they didn't have enough money to pay for all the groceries in their cart. Finally she just walked out, leaving her husband standing there, wondering what to do.

I had just finished paying for my order, and I said to my cashier, "I think they are short some money over there. Can you just use this to pay their bill?" I handed her my debit card (she's someone I know well!) and said, "I don't want to embarrass them. Just take this and I'll come back in half an hour to get it." And I walked out.

Older people, especially, are used to being independent, and they're so proud and embarrassed to accept help from anyone. That couple didn't need to know it was me. They just needed to know that somebody cared enough about them to make a difference. I don't know if I'll be able to do that forever, but while I can, I'm happy to do it. Besides, if I'm ever in need again, I surely hope somebody steps up and cares enough about me to make that kind of difference.

Please Don't Judge

I've mentioned a few times that if there's something you can get for free and it's not what you want or need, get it anyway and give it away. In my classes sometimes people resist that idea because, with food items especially, the kind of things you get for free are often prepackaged foods like Hamburger Helper. People say, "Well, that's not healthy

Helping Our Military Families

Earlier in the book I promised I'd tell you what to do with your expired coupons. Finally we're here! The commissaries at U.S. military bases overseas accept coupons up to six months after they've expired. These are coupons you're going to throw away. If you put them in an envelope and drop them in the mail instead, you can help military families save hundreds of thousands of dollars and have a huge impact on their lives.

I go through my coupon binder at the beginning of each month to take out all my expired coupons. You'll find several addresses of groups that collect and distribute these coupons at www.grocerysaving tips.com/expiredgrocerycoupons.htm and www .coupsfortroops.com. You can also contact your local American Legion to see if they ship coupons overseas. This is a wonderful way to support our military.

food, so I shouldn't be donating it." It might not be as healthy as organic chicken. But you know what? Nobody ever died from eating Hamburger Helper, but people do die from starvation. I can tell you, when my kids and I were hungry, I would have given anything to have a box of Hamburger Helper, and it sure is better than nothing at all in your stomach. So please, don't judge the food items.

Don't judge the people either. It's tempting to see people in need and think, They should go out and get a job! or They got themselves into this situation and need to get themselves out. Nobody ever gave me any handouts. But really, who are we to judge? We don't know what's going on in their lives or how they ended up where they are. Isn't it easier to be kind and generous, to give back and make a difference?

Another comment I hear in my couponing classes is "I gave to somebody, but they didn't appreciate it and they didn't thank me." That always makes me think back on my own experiences. I was so embarrassed about what I was going through those six months that my kids and I were alone. Nobody stepped up to help me, but if they had, I don't know how I would have responded. Not that I wouldn't have been appreciative, but I don't know if I would have been as gracious as they wanted me to be at that moment, out of embarrassment.

The people you help may be too embarrassed to show how much your gesture means to them. Or maybe they really don't feel that grateful because their life is just so very difficult. But maybe a few years down the road, when something else happens or they get out of whatever bad situation they're in, they might think, Oh my goodness, how wonderful that a total stranger stepped up and helped me when I really needed it.

Honestly, I feel that if we're giving because we want gratitude from somebody else, then we're really not giving with the right motive. The point of giving is to give freely and not expect anything in return. We just need to be generous. We need to think about other people instead of looking down on them and saying, "Well, they shouldn't be in this predicament." You know, we've all had times in our lives that we're not proud of. I know what it's like to have nothing, and the last thing I needed then was someone judging me. I already felt bad enough. It's so important to remember this when you see people in need. If everybody was positive and encouraged one another and lifted other people up, we could really make a difference and the world would be a much nicer place.

Nobody enjoys being on the receiving end of someone else's charity. It's such a humbling experience. That's why I helped out that older couple in the supermarket anonymously. Think about whether you have neighbors, and particularly older neighbors, who might be on a limited income and are much too proud to take any kind of assistance. Go over for a visit, and bring along something you got couponing. You can say, "You know, when I was at the grocery store I had this buy-one-get-one-free-coupon, but I really only need one. I hate to waste it; will you take the other one?" Then it doesn't seem like you thought they were needy. It's a double kindness to help them out in a way that allows them their dignity.

People who are ill or who are older might have trouble getting out and doing their grocery shopping or cooking as well. So cook up a little extra something for a neighbor in a separate pan. You can say something like "This recipe was just for too much for my family and there's no room left in the freezer. Can I give you the leftovers?" Then they think they're getting the leftovers, when really you planned to have enough to share.

Where Can You Donate?

When you're ready to donate, the next step is to figure out where. If you don't know of a food charity in your community, start with the local religious organizations/churches. Even if you are not affiliated with a particular church, you can call and ask, "Can you tell me where the local food banks are? I have items to donate." Churches and religious groups get calls all the time from people who need help, and even if they don't run their own food bank, they'll know where assistance is available. Organizations like the Salvation Army will also know about the food banks in your community.

You may have to make a few phone calls, but stick with it. Because you get so many things for free when you are couponing, it's often just a matter of donating a little bit of your time and energy to put that stuff in your car and drop it off at a food bank.

Don't be discouraged if you start by donating to a certain place but decide you don't really like it. Maybe they scruti-

Not Just Food

If you're struggling just to feed your family, you often end up making tough choices. Food comes first when the kids are hungry, and things like a new toothbrush or aspirin or sanitary products are lower on the list. You can't use food assistance to pay for those items either, so many families just do without.

That's why most food banks are happy to accept a lot more than food. I donate things like feminine products and toothpaste and toothbrushes, and every food bank has said to me, "Those are like gold, because families don't know how they would get them otherwise." These are the kinds of things you can almost always get for free when you're couponing, and you can really make a difference when you donate them.

nize what's given out, or are very restrictive about what items they accept, or some other reason. Remember, there are many, many places that are happy to receive your donations. Don't stop. Just make a few more calls and find another place where you are more comfortable giving.

When Disaster Strikes

A tornado, flood, or hurricane can devastate a community. When those kinds of disasters strike, disaster relief agencies always make appeals for funds. But you don't have to send money. You can send the items you gathered couponing and use all the money you've saved to pay for the shipping.

Of course you need to know where to send things. I usually start the same way as when I look for food banks—I call local churches. In a disaster, people go to their house of worship for help. Just go to your search engine, search for the city or town, and the Chamber of Commerce page will usually list the local places of worship. Make some calls and connect with a member of the clergy, who will be able to tell you what is needed and where to send it. You can also do a search for "name of the town" and something like "accepting food donations" or "accepting toiletries." On my blog, I post information after disasters so my couponing community can all pitch in and help. I invite all of you to join us.

Don't Forget the Animals

When disaster hits, the animal shelters are hit too. Even if they're not damaged, they're often inundated with pets who are suddenly homeless, and they desperately need dog and cat food and cat litter. If you don't have a pet but you're couponing, watch for deals on pet supplies and send what you can.

Even when there hasn't been a disaster, animal shelters are always overstretched. So when you find pet items for free, get them and donate them to your local shelter.

You may remember that terrible tornado in Tuscaloosa, Alabama, in 2011. I actually have family there, so I quickly got in touch with their church and sent a box of toiletries and personal hygiene stuff, which is usually what they're looking for after disasters like that. I put the name and address of the church on my blog and challenged everybody to box up five items and send them down there.

The church was nice enough to send some pictures back, showing how five items multiply. You think, It's just five little items, but when a thousand people send five items, that's a huge contribution to the disaster relief effort. So please, don't ever discount the size of your contribution. Even if you are only sending one thing, your one thing is going to have an impact on one person. And that is awesome!

My own community had a tornado two years ago and numerous families were displaced and lost everything. My friends and family went to the local church in the hardest hit part of town and picked up the tornado victims' dirty laundry (clothes that were blown out into the fields). I put out a request on my blog for donations of laundry detergent, spot remover, and dryer sheets. Then we went to a Laundromat owned by my friends David and Rosie Hadeed (Super Suds in Sylvania, Ohio), and they let us use all the washers and dryers for free.

Doing all the laundry for those displaced families meant a lot to them—and to us too. It was a great way to get a lot of people involved in whatever way they felt most comfortable. Some donated supplies, some donated their time washing and folding, and others donated their time to deliver the clothes back to the families. Each job was necessary to pull this off, so it all mattered. This goes to show once again that nobody can do great things alone. In this instance, more than fifty people joined together to make a difference in our community. Whether their individual contribution was large or small, it all added up to clean laundry for displaced families.

In chapter 8 I talked about how a stockpile can really save your family if there's a disaster. Your stockpile can also make it possible for you to save another family.

In March 2012, Indiana was hit by a string of deadly tornadoes that took out whole towns. One of the churches in the affected area contacted me because someone had seen me on *Extreme Couponing*. They needed food and personal hygiene items, and asked if I could help. I put the information on my blog and, as usual, challenged everybody to send five items. Most of the people who follow my blog have a stockpile, and I knew it would be easy for them to help out. People sent boxes and boxes of supplies. A lot of those who donated were on a tight budget themselves and could never have sent money. But because they had a stockpile, they were able to give back.

Having a stockpile also means you can donate whatever is most needed; you're not limited to what's on sale this week. In one particular relief effort, the biggest need might be food; in another it might be soap and shampoo. Whatever it is, you can take it right out of your stockpile.

Is This a Tax Deduction?

Considering all the items we give away from our open pantry, people often wonder, Do you claim it as a charitable deduction on your taxes? We don't. First of all, I'm getting the stuff for free or very cheap, so there's very little out-of-pocket expense for me. And we're giving because we personally believe it's the right thing to do. We're not doing it as a tax write-off.

Disasters aren't always big. Sometimes they affect just one family. A family in the town just up the road—a grandma and a grandpa who were raising their five grand-children—lost everything when their house burned down. They ended up living in a hotel with nothing, waiting for their insurance check. The superintendent at the kids' school contacted me and asked if I could help. So I sent a few boxes of things and put a notice on my blog.

The school principal later told me that one whole room of the school was filled with all the donations they got for this family. People who lived nearby also signed up to take them meals, and we ended up with enough volunteers for seven weeks. Couponers always have plenty of food, so making a meal for someone else doesn't cost much, but it shows you care.

It's such a good feeling, not only for the person receiv-ing, but for you as the giver. You know you're really helping someone who otherwise wouldn't have anything, affect-ing his or her life in a powerful way. And it's all simply be-cause you're using coupons. Who would have thought you could make such a huge difference with that little piece of paper?

Small Things Make a Big Difference

So many people think that in order to "count," your donation has to be something major. But sometimes the small things you do can make a huge difference in somebody's life. I have a nonprofit organization set up in memory of my mom, and around Christmastime we throw a party and give out presents to families who might not otherwise have much for Christmas. We get fun toys for the kids, but we also buy everyone packages of socks, shoes, coats, boots, bedding—the necessities, because I know how useful those can be.

About fifteen years ago, there was a little girl at one of the parties who didn't own a pair of socks. She was wearing mismatched socks that were hand-me-downs from her mom and were too big for her. When she opened her package of socks, she was so excited. "Look, Mom," she said, "just what I always wanted, my own socks!" I know a lot of kids wince when they get practical gifts like socks for Christmas, but for this little girl it was a very big deal.

Her mother told me that the eight-pack of socks was probably the gift her daughter was most excited about. Most people think a gift has to be extravagant to have that wow factor, but that package of socks affected this mom and her daughter, just because somebody cared enough to make sure her daughter had warm feet.

So that's what I mean. Giving just a smile, or an encouraging word to somebody, just being nice to somebody—it doesn't cost anything, but it means everything. I put a little devotion on my Facebook page every day as an encouragement, and many readers have e-mailed to say, "I really needed that today. I was having a bad day and that really puts life into perspective." And you know, it does.

I think it's easy to get discouraged because there is so much negativity around us. But you have to find the positive; when you do, your life will be a whole lot easier. Twenty years ago, when I was struggling to get by and nobody came to help me, I could have come out of it bitter and angry. But I've chosen to take a different path and to be the cheerleader and support for other people that I wished I'd had. I don't care who you are and what your circumstances are—you matter to me because you were put on this earth for a reason. If I can make a difference in your life, that's why God put me here.

One Person's Kindness

The world would be a much nicer place if everyone was simply kind to one another. On my trip to Las Vegas to film *Extreme Couponing All-Stars Finale*, I was reminded of how much impact the kindness—or lack of kindness—of just one person can have. I'm afraid to fly, and at first I didn't even want to go to Vegas. But eventually I agreed and took my oldest daughter, Ciera, with me, since Jamie had to stay home with our little ones.

When we got to the airport, my nerves really kicked in. The weather was windy and rainy, so I knew it was not going to be a smooth flight. As we started to board, my hands were sweating and my heart was racing. Then the pilot came on the loud-speaker to inform us that there would be a lot of tur-bulence. My daughter immediately turned to me and said, "It's okay, Mom," but I didn't feel that way!

A friend of ours is a pilot and told me I should let

the flight attendants know I am a nervous flier so they can keep an eye on me. So as we got to our seats, all the way in the back, I sat down and said to the flight attendant, "I am not a good flier." In a nasty tone, she replied, "Then, honey, this isn't the flight you want to be on." I immediately stood up and started to leave, my daughter following behind, saying, "Mom, you have to go to Vegas!" When we got to the front of the plane, the flight attendant and the pilot asked me what was going on. I said, "I don't fly well and the flight attendant in the back said this was not a flight I wanted to be on, so I am getting off." And I did.

I told my daughter to get back on the plane, because all our coupons were there, and that I would drive to Las Vegas and meet her. The problem was I needed to be there in eighteen hours, and the drive is thirty hours from where I live in Ohio. I wasn't sure how I was going to pull that off.

continued ...

I finally decided I had to fly, no matter how scared I was, and I talked to the gate agent. I ended up missing two other flights and finally got on the last flight of the day to Las Vegas. I sat down near the gate and was watching the woman taking tickets for the flight before mine. I thought, Wow, she is really nice. If only the flight attendant had been that nice, I might have stayed on the plane.

Well, after about fifteen minutes she walked up to me and said, "Can I ask you a silly question? Are you that lady from *Extreme Couponing*?" It felt so funny to be recognized, especially at an airport! She sat down next to me and we talked about couponing for a while. Then I told her I was heading to Las Vegas and was not a good flier, and I explained what happened with my earlier flight. She told me to wait a minute, checked the computer, and gave me a first-class seat. Yes, me in first class!

When the time came for my flight, she introduced me to all the flight attendants as they boarded the plane and explained how nervous I was. She also told them I was the lady from *Extreme Couponing*. I sat in first class and was treated like a queen. It was a smooth trip, and I will never forget Susan Fisher from Delta Airlines at Detroit Metro. She was truly my angel that day.

Lessons in Compassion

When we drop off supplies at the local food banks, our kids always come with us. My four younger ones weren't around when things were so hard for us, but the three older ones, of course, remember that terrible time. I don't want my younger four to ever experience that, but I do want them to know that not everyone has it as good as we do.

So they help out with the couponing and experience the thrill of getting lots and lots of stuff for very little money. But they also help out with taking what we get to food banks and putting it on the shelves. This way, they see both sides of couponing—what it enables us to get, and what it enables us to give.

The experience has made my children more compassionate and generous. My eight-year-old son, Jonah, came home from school one day and told me about a classmate who never seemed to have any lunch and was always saying he was hungry. Jonah said, "Mom, can we make up a bag of food for him? I'll put it in his backpack." I was so proud of him for thinking of a creative way to give this little boy food so he would not be embarrassed, and for knowing that he didn't need to be recognized for doing it!

Let's never be so focused on ourselves that we don't notice the needs of others. I want my children to understand, right from the start, what it means to be compassionate. And you know, when a compassionate heart becomes part of who you are, you really start listening to the needs of other people. Then you will understand how wonderful it is and how good it feels to help.

Takeaway Tip$

I'm Afraid I Can't Afford to Donate to Others.

If you're couponing, you're saving a bundle every week. Take a look in your stockpile and see what you have the most of. Donate a few of those items, and rebuild your stockpile when the price is right. Or concentrate on getting free items and then donate those. It costs you nothing!

I Can't Donate a Lot, So What Difference Does It Make?

None of us can do it alone, but when we all do something, the effect is enormous. When a hundred people donate one item, that's a hundred items. Never, ever underestimate your contribution. Someone will get your one item and know that someone cared. That's huge.

continued . . .

How Can I Find a Local Food Bank?

Start by calling the houses of worship and religious organizations in your town. If they don't run a food bank, they will know who does. When disaster strikes, you can find out where to send aid the same way. Get in touch with a local clergy member to find out what is most needed and where to send it.

Do Food Banks Accept Donations Other Than Food?

Most do. In fact, personal hygiene and cleaning supplies are often the most welcome because those are items families can't buy with food assistance. When a family has to choose between feeding hungry children and a tube of toothpaste, they choose the food. But they still need the toothpaste.

Why Can't the People Who Go to the Food Banks Just Get a Job and Get Their Lives Together?

You don't know what their circumstances are. Many people who have jobs still end up needing help from food banks. Others may have fallen into tough circumstances because of an accident or illness or just because times are hard. There's no reason to judge people—but there are plenty of reasons to help them!

Why Shouldn't I Throw Away My Expired Coupons?

The commissaries at U.S. military bases overseas accept coupons up to six months after they've expired. Expired coupons are no use to you anyway, so why not pop them in an envelope and send them to families who really need them?

CHAPTER 10

Living a
Frugal Life

My dad was a truck driver and my mom was a stay-at-home mom. They had four kids (I'm the baby), so my parents really knew how to stretch a dollar. At a very early age, we kids learned how much things cost and that you can't just spend money whenever you want to—you have to think about each and every purchase. Being frugal made it possible for my mom to stay home with us, which I am thankful for. I can remember us kids saving our pennies because my dad would always say, "Pennies make dollars." We saw that he was right too, and we learned never to discount the smallness of things. I know my dad would be very proud of me right now, living as frugally as I am and sharing money-saving strategies with all of you.

For me, being frugal has always been a way of life. Sometimes we're less frugal, and sometimes—like now, when Jamie is out of work—we're more frugal. But being frugal doesn't have to mean doing without. I know when times are tough, people think, Okay, I won't get a new winter coat, I can't get boots. I'll pass up the little extras like buying perfume or going out to dinner. In fact, you can have what you want if you are just more careful about how and when you shop for it.

Actually, by thinking and living frugally, you'll probably end up with more than you had before. Once you start changing your mind-set and your shopping habits in small ways, you'll be amazed how much further you can make a dollar go.

Spend less and have more: It's too good to be true, right? And we've always been taught that when something seems too good to be true, it probably is. But the tips I'll give you in this chapter really do work. I have tried them all myself and have been amazed!

We'll start with some of my favorite Web sites, and then we'll go out shopping and dining for a lot less than you probably imagined was possible.

Ebates

Honestly, when I discovered Ebates I thought, This is the greatest thing ever invented, because I'm getting paid to go shopping. Ebates (www.ebates.com) is a Web site that pays you back a percentage of all your online purchases. All you have to do is start your shopping trip at Ebates. From there, you go to the sites you normally shop at anyway, and get cash back from Ebates after your purchase.

It really does sound too good to be true, but it works. Last year I got fourteen hundred dollars back from Ebates. I'm not talking about a gift card or a store credit—they send you an actual check every three months that you take to the bank and cash or deposit it.

Here's how it works: You register at Ebates and pick a log-in name and a password. Then, every time you shop on the Internet, you log in to Ebates first. On their site you'll find a list of stores they're affiliated with, and the percentage of your purchase that you will get as cash back. There are more than a hundred online retailers affiliated with Ebates, including Amazon, Walmart, Drugstore.com, Apple, J.Crew, Sears, iTunes, Restaurant.com, and Lands' End.

When you've registered and are ready to start shopping, you just click on the name of the store you want to shop at, and you are redirected to the store's Web site. Ebates keeps track of how much you spend there, and puts the rebate amount in your account. In May, August, November, and February they mail you a check for whatever amount is in your account. You can also choose to have your rebate deposited in your PayPal account, if you have one, or to have your check sent to a charity or to a friend or family member. This is another great way to pass the blessing on.

Your rebate can range from one percent all the way up to ninety percent of a purchase when there is a special promotion. Or sometimes it will be a flat amount, like five dollars. There are frequent promotions, such as double your cash back if you shop at certain stores. There are also online coupons that get you special deals by typing in a promotion code when you check out at the online store.

There are a lot of deals and coupons and promotions on Ebates, and if you find them a little overwhelming, that's okay. Just ignore them if you prefer. If all you do is go to the box that lists Ebates affiliates—it's in the upper left side of the home page—and click through to your shopping destination, you're still going to save a bundle.

Yes, you have to wait three months to get your rebate, but you're not paying anything extra to shop through Ebates, so that's just found money, like when you find money in your pocket you didn't know was there. Bonus! Around Christmastime, the rebates for some sites really go up. That means in February you'll be getting a nice check to offset some of your December spending, or to start the new year with some extra cash.

Smell Sweet for Less

If you like really expensive perfumes or colognes, Scentiments (www.scentiments.com) is a neat find (and it's an Ebates affiliate). The site sells the genuine article, but the bottles come without the fancy box. Usually they're bottles of perfume that were meant to be testers—the open bottles in the store that are set

continued ...

out so people can try a little of the scent. Stores open more tester bottles than they actually use, but they can't sell the perfume without the original box. Those bottles—unopened and unused—end up on Scentiments, selling at a steep discount.

Last year I got my daughter a bottle of Dolce & Gabbana perfume for Christmas. It's usually a hundred dollars, and I got her a brand-new bottle for fifty dollars. She didn't mind at all that it wasn't in the original box—what she wanted was the perfume. And as I told her, "For an extra fifty dollars I could have gone to the store and gotten you the box, but I thought you'd rather have the fifty dollars to spend on something else you want."

Swagbucks

Swagbucks (www.swagbucks.com) is another site that rewards you for surfing the Internet, which most of us do anyway. When you download the Swagbucks toolbar, you earn points for doing things like searching the Internet, taking surveys, shopping online, and playing games on your computer. Some of these activities you access through the Swagbucks home page, and some earn you rewards no matter where you are on the Internet.

You can trade in the points for goods or gift cards. There are things you don't need a lot of points for, such as five-dollar gift cards for Target and Amazon, and things you can save up your points for, such as audio equipment. Look through the rewards Swagbucks offers and decide if you want to save up your points for something big or cash them in for lots of small things. I bank my gift cards in my Amazon account and then use the money at Christmastime.

More Discount Goodies

Saveology (www.saveology.com) is another favorite Web site of mine. They offer discounts on a huge variety of goods—everything from wristwatches to cosmetics to pet supplies—plus deals on restaurants and sporting events in some cities. They also offer gift cards for places like JCPenney, Macy's, Build-A-Bear, and CVS, discounted at

Christmastime to between ten dollars and fifteen dollars for a twenty-five-dollar gift card. So that's at least a forty percent discount.

Freeflys

Freeflys (www.freeflys.com) is a Web site that finds offers for free samples from all over the Internet and pulls them together in one place. Once you register on Freeflys, you can search their offers for food, health, beauty, children's, and household products. Freeflys will tell you how to get the offer and then redirect you to the Internet site where you can get what you want. Your sample comes in the mail, usually in a couple of weeks.

If you like, you can subscribe to Freeflys's daily offers, e-mails that say, "Do you want this free sample?" (just click yes or no). Freeflys also has a link to Internet printable coupons.

Each month there's anywhere from twenty to thirty products on offer, and you request just the ones you want. Normally it's just the small trial size, although very occasionally you'll get a full-size product. But still, it's free. Nine times out of ten it will come with a high-value coupon as well—a dollar off or even more. So if you like the product, you'll get a deal on a full-size package.

To get the free sample, you may have to "like" the manufacturer's page on Facebook, or register on a manufacturer's Web site, or enter a contest, or write a few sentences about an experience you've had. If any of those things seem like too much trouble, stick to the offers that only require you to give the manufacturer your name and address. You'll find there are still plenty of free samples to choose from.

Offers on Freeflys are usually for newer products. For example, when Tide came out with a laundry detergent packet called Pods, they sent out free samples good for one load of laundry. On my blog a lot of people complained about the fact that they could do only one load with the sample, but I said, "Give it to a food bank, then, because a lot of families would love to be able to do one load of laundry for free."

Actually, these kinds of samples are a great way to get items to donate. If you don't need the product, give it to someone who does. If you don't need the coupon, pass that on as well. It hasn't cost you anything, and it's such an easy way to give back.

Giving Out Your Address

To get a free sample, you have to send the company your mailing address. Otherwise, where are they going to mail your sample?

If you don't feel comfortable doing that, then free samples are not for you. Honestly, though, I've never had a problem with it. I only sign up for samples from the manufacturer's site or through offers on Freeflys. I don't give out other information, such as my phone number. And legitimate companies will never ask for sensitive information like a bank account number or Social Security number.

Facebook

Many of the promotions listed on Freeflys send you to the manufacturer's Facebook page to get your sample. Typically, you have to "like" the product—just click the button that says "like" at the top of the page.

Companies have all kind of promotions, contests, give-aways, and coupons when you like them on Facebook. For example, last year on Oscar Mayer's Facebook page you could print a dollar-off coupon for any hot dog or lunch meat. Then they asked you to give what they called a "tastimonial"—a sentence or two about why you like their hot dogs or lunch meat—to receive another coupon. The more people who gave "tastimonials," the higher the coupon value. The last time I looked, the coupon was up to five dollars off!

Chain restaurants will sometimes send you a coupon for a free food item, and you can also get free samples this way. Companies do these promotions so that people will follow them on Facebook. It keeps them in the social media network and connected with their customers. To take part, you have to sign up for Facebook (www.facebook .com). When you've set up your account, go to the search box at the top of any Facebook page and search for the name of companies whose products you like or want to try. Click on a company's name and Facebook will take you there.

And as long as you're on Facebook, come and visit me

at https://www.facebook.com/pages/Saving-and-Sharing-for-Christ/123889597686086. We have a lot of fun on the Facebook page and everyone is very encouraging and uplifting—plus, you will find a lot of great deals there.

Tell Us What You Think

I love it when people ask my opinion, and surveys are a way I can get paid to sound off. Survey companies want to know what consumers think about a wide range of things, and they'll pay you for your opinions. When you sign up with a survey company, you tell them some things about yourself, such as your gender, age, and ethnicity, and then every week they e-mail you a link to a survey you can take.

Often the surveys are about products, so sometimes they'll send you a sample first. Last summer I tried a new kind of laundry detergent, and the survey asked questions like "Do you like the smell?" and "Do you think it got your clothes clean?" Your opinions help the manufacturer determine whether it's a good product and if people will buy it.

Another kind of survey I see fairly often is one that tries

to determine what kinds of products sell better at different times of the year. So a survey might ask if you bought a lawn mower or a TV or a computer in the past month. Others ask you about what brands you look for and how brand loyal you are. Your honest opinion is valuable because it helps companies improve their products as well as how they market them. You might even see surveys about advertisements, where they show you an ad they're thinking about running and ask things like "Did this catch your attention? Did you notice this particular part? When you saw the picture, what stuck out most for you?"

Some days I might not get any surveys; some days I might get three. One day I got five surveys. Some of them are extremely short; some of them are long. One company sometimes sends a survey that takes as long as forty-five minutes to complete. But for that one, you get a fifty-dollar gift card. Fifty dollars for forty-five minutes' work? That's more than a dollar a minute!

The survey companies pay you in lots of different ways. With some, you earn points that can be redeemed for rewards—gifts cards or merchandise. Some actually give you cash that you can put into an Amazon account or your

PayPal account. They will tell you before you sign up for any surveys exactly how the rewards will be paid.

It's all free money, which means I'm not going into debt at Christmastime or when my kids go back to school, so it's worth it to me. Last year, I earned more than two thousand dollars in credits and gift cards. I ended up buying three really nice North Face winter coats and a Kindle with my survey money, and paid about $2.52 out of pocket for everything.

Tried-and-True Survey Companies

There are a lot of survey companies out there, but I haven't tried them all. Here's a list of the ones I have tried. You can always find an up-to-date list on my blog. Go to www.FreeTastesGood.com. On the right-hand sidebar, down toward the bottom, you'll find a box that says "Survey Companies." These are survey firms I have used myself, so I know they're legit.

☐ Opinion Outpost (www.opinionoutpost.com)
☐ Inbox Dollars (www.inboxdollars.com)

- ☐ i-Say (www.i-say.com)
- ☐ MyView (portal.myview.com)
- ☐ MindField Online (mindfieldonline.com)
- ☐ NPD Online Research (www.npdor.com)
- ☐ Opinion Place (www.opinionplace.com)
- ☐ Vindale Research (www.vindale.com)
- ☐ Univox (univoxcommunity.com)
- ☐ Consumer Advisory Group (www.consumer advisorygroup.com)
- ☐ Valued Opinions (www.valuedopinions.com)

The gift cards you earn may not be for places where you usually shop. In fact, someone complained to me recently that one of the survey companies only offers gift cards for Macy's. Well, there are a lot of nice things at Macy's. And remember, everything you get with that gift card is free for you. Sometimes people don't like the fact that it takes about thirty days to get your gift card. But to me, it doesn't matter if it takes a month. Fifty dollars is still fifty dollars.

Another kind of survey you might see shows up on your

register receipt. Stores like Dick's Sporting Goods, Rite Aid, JCPenney, Gap, and Banana Republic have these. On the receipt will be a request that you call a phone number or visit a Web site and answer a few questions about your shopping experience, such as how good the service was. In return you'll receive a discount code or an OYNO coupon. Sometimes they're good for as much as twenty percent off your next purchase.

Out on the Town

It's time to step away from your computer and get out of the house! Two of the services I like a lot for discounts on all kinds of fun things—from restaurants to concerts to spas to weekend getaways to full vacations—are Groupon (www .groupon.com) and Living Social (www.livingsocial.com). After you register, and tell them a little bit about what you like, you will receive offers every day for deals such as twenty dollars for forty dollars' worth of food at a particular restaurant or twelve dollars for a fifty-dollar haircut at a specific salon in your neighborhood. You purchase only the deals you're interested in. When you do, you get a voucher that you take to the place of business. The vouchers do expire in a couple of months, but you will always know before you buy how long the deal is good for.

You'll usually save at least fifty percent off the regular price of what you're buying. This is a great way to get to know new restaurants and other businesses in your town. You can also search for vouchers in other cities, for when you are traveling.

Restaurant.com (www.restaurant.com) is another great place to find discount restaurant vouchers. You can get gift certificates for local restaurants at discounts that range from thirty percent to fifty percent and more. Go to the Web site through Ebates and you'll do even better. Read the fine print, though, because while you can sometimes get a twenty-five-dollar voucher for less than a dollar, it often says you have to spend at least thirty-five dollars at the restaurant. That means your actual out-of-pocket expenses for thirty-five dollars' worth of food would be ten dollars—still a huge savings.

Around Christmastime, Restaurant.com gift certificates usually pay seventy percent back on Ebates. So if I buy a ten-dollar gift card, I'll eventually get seventy percent of that back—seven dollars—which means the gift card cost me only three dollars.

Gift Cards—A Gift for You Too

There's a supermarket near me that has a gas station attached to it, and for every fifty dollars you spend, you get ten cents off a gallon of gas, up to thirty gallons. That's a nice deal, but here's what's even nicer: Every June, if you buy a fifty-dollar gift card at the supermarket, you get quadruple gas perks—forty cents off every gallon. Forty cents multiplied by thirty gallons is twelve. So if I buy a gift card for someone as a graduation present, I get twelve off my gas. They get the present, I get the savings. Pretty sweet, right?

And it's not like the gift card is for shopping at the supermarket. There are all sorts of gift cards for sale there, for all kinds of stores and restaurants, iTunes, and a lot more, including Visa gift cards, which can be used any place Visa credit cards are accepted. Take a look at what your supermarket offers; you might be surprised.

You could even buy a gift card for yourself. If I buy a fifty-dollar gift card in June, it's really only costing me thirty-eight dollars, because I'm getting twelve dollars off on gas—and I have to buy gas anyway.

Many supermarkets are associated with gas stations, and most of them offer you some kind of discount on your gas when you shop at the store, so definitely look into it.

Building a Gift Card Bargain

I recently put together a great deal on sunscreen. Target had a dollar-off coupon; plus, I had a two-dollars-off manufacturer's coupon, and on top of that, for every two bottles you bought, you got a five-dollar Target gift card. The sunscreen was $4.98, or $9.96 for two. I stacked two Target coupons (a dollar off each, for a total of two dollars off) with two manufacturers' coupons (two dollars off each, for a total of four dollars off). So all together, I got six dollars off and paid $3.96 for those two bottles of sunscreen; I also got a five-dollar Target gift card, so when you think about it, Target paid me a dollar four to buy those two bottles of sunscreen!

Jamie and I head a nonprofit organization that we started in memory of my mom to help less fortunate families at Christmas. Two years ago we went to the supermarket and purchased all the gift cards we needed to buy the items from the children's Christmas lists. Because of the store's gift card offer, we earned so many fuel perks that we didn't have to pay for gas for three and a half months.

Here's how it works, at least at our local Kroger. When we buy the gift card at the store, the store scans our Kroger savings card. Then, when we go to the gas station attached to the Kroger, we scan our savings card again and it automatically gives us the savings. Last year alone, we saved twelve hundred dollars in gas by doing that, and that was just at Kroger. It definitely adds up and it doesn't take much preparation to save like that.

If you don't have a car, gift cards can still work for you. For example, around the holidays many drugstore chains offer discounts on gift cards, for example, a twenty-five-dollar gift card for twenty dollars. That's twenty percent off. You can buy those gift cards as gifts for others, but remember you can also buy them for yourself. Why bother? Because then everything you buy with that gift card is twenty percent off. You've paid twenty dollars and you're getting twenty-five dollars' worth of stuff. Who doesn't want five dollars for doing practically nothing?

Winter in the Spring—Buying out of Season

Great deals come to those who wait. Last December a woman posted on my Facebook page asking where she could get the best deal on a new artificial Christmas tree. I told her to wait until after Christmas, when she could save at least seventy-five percent and get a great new tree for next year. Yes, there were twenty-five-percent-off deals before Christmas, but why not cover up those bare spots on the old tree with popcorn chains, wait a few weeks, and save three times as much?

The same with winter coats. If you take yours out of the closet in November and think it looks a little shabby, get out the needle and thread, or wear an extra sweater to keep warm, and wait until January when all the winter clothes go on sale. Every time you do that, you'll save twenty, thirty, or even more. Save thirty dollars on thirty items throughout the year and you've saved nine hundred dollars!

Season	What's on Sale
Early January	Toys, Christmas trees, decorations, cards
January/February	Winter coats, boots, sweaters, snow shovels, snow blowers
March	Snow shovels, snow blowers, rock salt
April/May	Easter decorations and baskets, fancy clothes for kids
July/August	Barbecue grills and supplies, swimming pool toys and supplies, outdoor furniture, swimsuits, summer clothes
September/October	Back-to-school clothes, school supplies, gardening supplies

The key is to shop the end-of-season sales. And in fact, the retailers are making it easier and easier for you to do that, because the seasons seem to be ending earlier. For example, summer clothes used to go on sale in late August, early September. Now they go on sale in the middle to end of July, when you still have plenty of summer left.

Stockpiling comes into play here too. So, for example, when you shop the back-to-school sales in mid- to late September, stock all the school supplies your kids will need to take them right through the school year and into the start of the next school year. All the stuff is fifty to seventy-five percent off, and it keeps forever. Then the kids can just take what they need all year from the stockpile, and you can stock up again the following September.

You can stockpile clothes too. You basically know how much your kids grow every year, so if you buy them new winter coats in January, you can get them one size larger so they have room to grow, and then put the coats away for next winter. As with all stockpiling, you have to lay out some money when you stock up, but it really stretches your dollar in the long run.

The Gift Closet

One of the things I stock up on right after Christmas is toys and other gifts. I always buy an assortment of things for boys and girls of a variety of ages. I stay away from whatever the fad toy is at the moment and stick with perennial favorites like LEGOs and dolls.

I pick up all the toys and gifts when they're seventy-five percent off, and put them in the gift closet. Then when the kids are invited to birthday parties or other gift-giving events, they go shopping in the gift closet and pick out what they think is most appropriate. This way, they have plenty of nice things to choose from for their friends and we never have to pay full price.

Everything in the gift closet is brand-new and unopened, and is actually a bit nicer than what we'd be buying if we had to pay full price. Last January we really stocked up on cute girly things. One of my daughters was invited to ten parties during the year, and she was able to make up wonderful gift bags with all the things we had in the gift closet. She made lots of little girls happy for hardly any money, but they had no idea. (Now my secret is out!)

Mindful Shopping

Sometimes when you want something, it feels like an itch you just have to scratch—*right now*! But a key part of living frugally is learning how to wait for the best deal before you buy. You need to get away from the typical shopping scenario, where you decide you want an iPod, so you run out to the nearest store and get it today. Because that's when everything costs the most. If you wait until the right deal comes along, you could probably buy two iPods for the same price.

It's not always easy to wait for what you want. But once you do, and see how much you can save, you'll start feeling so good about it that it will become a habit. It's just amazing how much you can get—and how much money you'll have left—when you become a mindful shopper.

Sometimes, when you wait for what you want, you also realize that you don't want it as much as you thought you did. If you don't scratch that itch the instant it arises, while you're waiting for the right deal you have time to think it over. So many people pick something up on impulse, and then a week later wonder, What was I thinking? I just spent three hundred dollars on this and I don't really need it. When you plan to buy something, though, it gives you time to consider whether it's really something you've got to have.

If it is, go ahead and get it. But get it at the best price that you can.

Really, frugal living is about getting what you need at a price you can truly afford. And to do that, you need to plan and to think about the long term. The more you think only about what you want today and what you are spending today, the more likely you are to overstretch yourself financially.

I hope you don't come to the end of this book thinking extreme couponing is about getting more and more stuff. Really, it's about being more thoughtful in the way you get stuff. Is it truly a smart investment? Is it really something you need? Because there's a big difference between needing something and wanting something. If you want it, that's okay too, but take the time to plan your purchase out just right. Shop mindfully, consciously. Shop with a plan. You'll have what you need, and what you really want, and your family won't be in debt to do it.

Takeaway Tip$

Aren't All Those Internet Shopping and Survey Deals Just Too Good to Be True?

Luckily for us, they're good *and* true! Companies really will pay you just for shopping, because stores want a way to direct you to their Web sites. Manufacturers will pay you for your opinions, because they use them to make their products and their marketing campaigns more appealing. And companies will send you free samples because they want you to try their products, buy them again, and tell your friends. Likewise, the merchants who sign up for discount programs like Groupon and Living Social want you to come to their business once, because they hope then you'll come again and again. These are all legitimate programs; you just need to tap into them to start saving big.

Is It Dangerous for Me to Give Out My Address to a Company over the Internet?

If a company is going to mail you a coupon or a free product or a rebate check, they need to know where to mail it. Your address is a matter of public record anyway—it may even be in the phone book. As long as you don't give out more sensitive information, you'll be fine.

continued . . .

What If I End up with Gift Cards and Rewards for Stores I Don't Shop At?

Buy yourself a present. Or else give the gift card away as a present, donate it, or use it to buy things you donate.

What's Wrong with Buying Things on Impulse?

You almost never get the best price when you decide you want something and then just run out and buy it that day. If you wait for a sale and make a plan, you're much more likely to get exactly what you want *and* have money left over as well. Waiting to make a purchase also gives you time to think about what you really want, as opposed to what tickles you at the moment.

Is Frugal Living About Doing Without Some Things?

Absolutely not. Frugal living is about having everything you need at a price you can afford. It's about thinking long-term and understanding that small savings add up to big advantages. When you plan what you're going to buy and when you're going to buy it, you're able to get the lowest possible price. And that means your dollar will stretch further than you ever thought possible. You'll have what you need, you'll have what you want, and you'll have enough left over to help others!

Happy Couponing, everyone!

ACKNOWLEDGMENTS

I would like to dedicate this book to my dad and Aunt Barb.
To Dad, thank you for teaching me the importance of
stretching *every* penny, because pennies make dollars, so
don't discount their smallness. I so wish I could have taken
you on a "couponing road trip." I love and miss you, Dad!

To my aunt Barb: Thank you for showing me at a very
young age that our wealth does not come from earthly pos-
sessions, but our greatest treasures come from our richness
in the Lord.

God: Thank you for placing on my heart at the very
young age of five the importance of feeding the hungry, being compassionate, and loving others as you love me. Thank
you for opening doors for me thirty-five years later and re-
vealing to me how, through the power of coupons, I could

feed hundreds of thousands of people! I will continue to do my best to make a difference in this world all for your glory.

To my husband, Jamie, and seven wonderful children: Thank you for loving me and standing beside me on this "couponing journey." Jamie, thanks for supporting me and being just as passionate as I am about this couponing ministry and feeding the hungry. Ciera, Cliff, and Lara, I am so sorry we had to endure what we did when you were so young, but through that trial God has opened up so many opportunities for us and has taught us the value of money and the importance of giving, and opened our hearts and minds to be generous to others. To my four youngest—Isaiah, Jonah, Josiah, and Jadyn—I'm so glad you know the importance of giving to the less fortunate and feeding the hungry. I love you all and am blessed beyond measure by each of you.

To Beth Adelman: Working with you has been absolutely wonderful. Thank you for all your kindness and conveying the passion for my ministry in this book. I am sure we will be lifetime friends.

Discovery Communication, New American Library, Erin, Niki, and Dustin from TLC: Thank you for believing in me and giving me this wonderful opportunity. My prayer is that this book will change lives and help others to save money all while *passing the blessing on!* There truly is power in coupons. None of this would have been possible if you all did not believe in me. Thank you!

To my dear friend Jen Moyer Geiger: Thank you for spending endless hours with me reading and rereading each chapter of this book to add those special touches so my personality came through, and thanks for always encouraging me. I love you and your friendship means the world to me.

To Rachel Szykowny: Thank you for showing me how to get two items for free with coupons. I bet you never imagined I would take it to this level. You're the best!

To Sharp Entertainment: Rebecca, Jason, Jeff, Martin, Ian, Nicole, Kiran, and the rest of the gang, thank you for believing in me and giving me so many opportunities on *Extreme Couponing.* You will always be considered "family." I love you guys!

To my sister, Karen, thank you for being my bestest friend and the best sister in the world. I love you and am hoping this book will finally help you learn how to coupon, LOL!

My family and church family: Thank you for all your countless prayers and encouragement during my life and through this journey. I would not be who I am today without your love, support, and most important, your prayers.

Mike and Mary Beam: Thank you for *always* encouraging me, supporting me, and praying for me. You have been two of my biggest encouragers and I will always be grateful to the both of you. Love you both bunches!

To the Coupontourage—Danielle, Vanessa, Dottie, Amy, and Tiffany: Thank you for planning and going on the shops with me as well as making others aware of the importance of giving back. You guys have always encouraged me and stood beside me. You are the best friends ever. I couldn't do it without you. I love you! *Holla-lujah!*

Mary Beth and Rick—WRVF FM 101.5, The River, Toledo, Ohio: What can I say but thank you from the bottom of my heart? You have given me so many opportunities to share my ministry. You *always* make me smile and laugh each week. I love you both so much and am thankful for all the opportunities you have given me.

Tim and Jeff in the morning—KMCK 105.7, Fayetteville, Arkansas: My two coupie buddies, thank you for showing others that "real men *do* coupon for feminine hygiene products," because it makes a difference and changes lives. I love you both, and your support has been amazing. You guys *rock*! Toledo misses you!

To our local news channels, WTVG 13 and WTOL 11, and the *Toledo Free Press*—Kristian Brown and Jack, Kelly Heidbreder, Wendy, Nicole, Craig Thomas, Chris Vickers, Melissa, Tom Pounds, and Michael Miller: Thank you for all your support, airtime, and the opportunity to share my message with so many people in the Toledo area. I am blessed to live in such a kind, caring community where making a difference matters.

Fitness 4 All and Justin: Thank you for helping me stay in shape while writing this book and getting ready for my photo shoot on the back cover. When others thought I couldn't do it, you guys believed in me!

To Hope Tabernacle Church in New Jersey: Thank you for believing in my ministry and what I am doing. Thank you for your continued prayers and helping me get my message out there. Matthew 25:40—all for the Glory of God!

To all the FB fans and blog followers: None of this would have been possible without your support and prayers. You guys are the best and I am blessed beyond measure by all of you. Ready, set, coupon!

Heather Moritz (www.MoritzFineDesigns.com) and Brandon (www.MyWpExpert.com): Thank you for all your hard work on my blog and getting it looking *awesome* while I was spending so much time on the book! You two are amazing.

To Ellen DeGeneres and Tim Tebow: I am sending you both a copy of this book and hope that you will be inspired to help me feed the hungry. With your star power and my coupon knowledge, we could feed so many people and change communities . . . one coupon at a time! Have your people call my people (okay, they can call me).

Lastly, if one life is changed or one person is encouraged by this book, then it was a success to me. I hope many of you will join me in saving and sharing!